PRAISE FOR Life in the Balance

This is not a time for Christians to sit and wring their hands. Christians, living up to the highest ideals of their faith, have always defended the weak and vulnerable and eagerly worked to strengthen the vital institutions of civil society. Joni Eareckson Tada and her team work tirelessly for the equal protection of every innocent human being at every stage of development and in every condition. In *Life in the Balance,* they equip the Church to think biblically about these issues. It's where the rubber meets the road. It is where the battle really is joined.

Chuck Colson
Founder of Prison Fellowship and The Chuck Colson Center
for Christian Worldview

In *Life in the Balance,* Joni and Friends provide an unflinching look at complex cultural and global issues surrounding the sanctity of life and how we as God's people can think about these hot topics. Stories of oppression, abuse, depression, neglect and disability showcase the way God redeems even the darkest hours to inform, change and grow us when we submit to His eternal perspective. I have seen firsthand how the themes of this book have been lived out in Joni's courageous leadership through Joni and Friends, at Biola University, and throughout the world.

Barry Corey
President, Biola University, La Mirada, CA

When Joni speaks, I listen. What Joni writes, I read. When she commends the insights of like-minded friends, I pay attention. And so should you. Unable to run here and there with perfectly formed limbs, Joni has spent countless hours contemplating *Life in the Balance*. As her life has grown richer and deeper, she has been empowered to bless multitudes out of the overflow of a life spent in the presence of the Master.

Hank Hanegraaff
President of the Christian Research Institute
Host of the *Bible Answer Man* Broadcast

Life in the Balance poses a crucial question: What do you say when faced with one of life's "sticky dilemmas"—those hot button, complex social issues of our day? How do you respond when those difficult questions enter your own life? Abortion, autism, the stem cell debate . . . these issues and more are examined through the lens of Scripture, practical application, and reasoned scientific information. And who better to lead this timely discussion than my good friend Joni Eareckson Tada? Decades in a wheelchair have given her wisdom, knowledge, insight and compassion for such a time as this. Joni and her friends have done the Christian community a valuable service in compiling this heart-and-soul-challenging book.

Max Lucado
Pastor and Bestselling Author of *Outlive Your Life*

If you are anything like me—and in this case I suspect you are—reading a comprehensive book on bioethics is not on your "bucket list" of things to do in life. Most of us can barely begin to grasp all of the biblical, philosophical, moral, scientific and emotionally personal issues related to the ethics of birth, life and death. Yet humanity cannot afford for the followers of Jesus Christ to sit on the sidelines while scientific developments and "survival of the fittest" values race forward!

As a pastor, I have struggled to get my own head and heart around these sensitive issues—let alone to help others grapple with them. *Life in the Balance* ended that for me! This captivating book tackles the toughest issues related to bioethics and disability. Joni and her team all bring tremendous credibility to the areas about which they each write. They are not merely theorists but also individuals who have faced these issues personally. They graciously weave heart-wrenching personal stories, scientific information, biblical truths and practical applications into an easily understood resource for all. Ultimately, each reader will be challenged to value every human life, from conception to death, as fearfully and wonderfully made by God Himself!

Shawn Thornton
Senior Pastor, Calvary Community Church, Westlake Village, CA
www.calvarycc.org

Joni Eareckson Tada
& F R I E N D S

Biblical Answers for the Issues of Our Day

LIFE IN THE
BALANCE

Regal

From Gospel Light
Ventura, California, U.S.A.

Published by Regal
From Gospel Light
Ventura, California, U.S.A.
www.regalbooks.com
Printed in the U.S.A.

Library of Congress Cataloging-in-Publication Data
Life in the balance : biblical answers for the issues of our day
/ Joni Eareckson Tada & friends.
p. cm.
Includes bibliographical references (p.   ) and index.
ISBN 978-0-8307-5520-2 (hardcover)
1. Christian life. 2. Christian ethics. 3. Christianity and culture.
I. Tada, Joni Eareckson.
BV4501.3.L5415 2010
261.8—dc22
2010016930

Rights for publishing this book outside the U.S.A. or in non-English languages are administered by Gospel Light Worldwide, an international not-for-profit ministry. For additional information, please visit www.glww.org, email info@glww.org, or write to Gospel Light Worldwide, 1957 Eastman Avenue, Ventura, CA 93003, U.S.A.

To order copies of this book and other Regal products in bulk quantities, please contact us at 1-800-446-7735.

Lovingly dedicated to
Margie Trimble and Carroll Brown.
Thank you for your legacy, which is
securing the lives of the weakest
and most vulnerable for the kingdom of
Christ around the world.

Contents

Acknowledgments 9

Foreword *by Chuck Colson* 10

1. Life's Sticky Dilemmas 12
   By Joni Eareckson Tada

2. When Life Isn't Fair: Violence in the Streets 33
   By Joni Eareckson Tada

3. Making Sense of Autism 53
   By Pat Verbal

4. Self-Image in a Fickle Culture 72
   By Joni Eareckson Tada

5. Searching for the Greater Good: The Stem Cell Debate.......92
   By Joni Eareckson Tada

6. The Truth Behind the Pain of Abortion 110
   By Sheila Harper

7. A Calloused Conscience: Eugenics and Genocide................130
   By Joni Eareckson Tada

8. From Obscurity to Celebrity by Way of Tragedy:
   End-of-Life Issues 150
   By Kathy McReynolds

9. I've Got Questions About the American Dream 170
   By Steve Bundy

10. Now What?..192
    By Joni Eareckson Tada

Appendix A: The Manhattan Declaration 211

Appendix B: Glossary of Terminology 217

Appendix C: Recommended Resources 224

Appendix D: Joni and Friends International
             Disability Center 226

Endnotes 229

Contributors 233

Scripture Index 237

Acknowledgments

A special thanks to all the wonderful friends and families who shared their lives in this *Life in the Balance* book and DVD. For all the times you hurdle each challenge, for all the grace and dignity you show though you are weary and worn, for the times you face the jaws of suffering and refuse to give in or give up, may God's favor and grace be yours. Thank you for inspiring and encouraging us through your heaven-blessed stories!

Foreword

If you're like me, you often read the morning newspaper and shake your head in disbelief. You're shocked at how our society appears to be spinning off its moral axis toward an uncertain abyss. This is not a time for Christians to sit and wring their hands.

That's why Joni Eareckson Tada and her team at the Joni and Friends International Disability Center are on the frontline of some of the hottest issues of our day. I'm glad to have the opportunity to tell you how supportive I am of this cutting-edge ministry.

One of the great dangers in our society today is that we are minimizing the importance of human life. Of course, we all know the debate about abortion—this debate has been front and center for 30 years, as well it should be. But the assault on human life spreads way beyond the abortion issue. The moment we begin to say that we want to do the greatest good for the greatest number of people; the moment we want utilitarian ethics to guide our decisions, then people get marginalized. People on the fringes of our society get lost and forgotten.

I am personally sensitive to this issue because of the work I have done in prisons all these years. But I'm especially concerned about what's happening in our society, because I have an 18-year-old grandson who has autism. While public opinion has moved in a prolife direction, powerful and determined forces are working to expand abortion, embryo-destructive research, assisted suicide and euthanasia. Although protecting the weak and vulnerable is the first obligation of government, the power of today's government is investing in causes that promote a "culture of death."

So I salute Joni and her team for the work they do at the Joni and Friends International Disability Center. I applaud their Christian Institute on Disability for promoting the sanctity of all human life. They tirelessly work for the equal protection of every innocent human being at every stage of development and in every condition. The Christian Institute on Disability continues to equip the church to think biblically about the issue of life, for that's what is really at stake. It's where the rubber meets the road. It is where the battle really is joined. Are we going to care for all people and ascribe to them their innate dignity in life? Yes! Not because the elderly, the disabled and the unborn possess certain rights, but because they have a God-given dignity. We affirm that we will not marginalize the people in our society who are the weakest.

Christians, living up to the highest ideals of their faith, have always defended the weak and vulnerable and eagerly worked to protect and strengthen vital institutions of civil society, beginning with the family. It was in this tradition that I, and a group of prominent Christian clergy, ministry leaders, and scholars, released the Manhattan Declaration on November 20, 2009, at a press conference in Washington, DC. The 4,700-word declaration speaks in defense of the sanctity of life, traditional marriage and religious liberty. It issues a clarion call to Christians to adhere firmly to their convictions in these three areas. I encourage all of you to read the Manhattan Declaration and affirm this important declaration of conscience.

Finally, I thank God for Joni Eareckson Tada and the tremendous work the International Disability Center and its Christian Institute on Disability are doing. God bless Joni and Friends, and God bless you.

Chuck Colson
Founder of Prison Fellowship
The Chuck Colson Center for Christian Worldview

Life's Sticky Dilemmas

By Joni Eareckson Tada

As never before in human history, we're bombarded with news stories about people facing physical and emotional crises that result in lifelong suffering. Many of these dilemmas are compounded by ethical conflicts, medical technology and social injustices. It is so overwhelming that we can become calloused—until it hits home. Then we cry out for answers, but we won't find them on CNN. Only God's Word offers solutions to our world's most pressing questions. God's Word is the source of truth! I've written a lot of books and am grateful to God for the ministry each one has had in the lives of thousands of readers. But this book may be one of the most important I've worked on. Let me tell you why.

The other day, while having coffee with my friend Shirley, our conversation turned to the unlikely subject of people in comas. Six months earlier, her cousin had suffered a severe stroke and has yet to respond. With hopes for a full recovery quickly diminishing, and health insurance nearly depleted, Shirley explained that her cousin was yet again transferred to another nursing home. This one was more of a state-subsidized warehouse for "hopeless cases." My friend looked at me with doleful eyes. "What would *you* say to the family, Joni?"

It happens to me more often than it used to . . . questions like that. And they're not just about the end-of-life implications of someone in a coma. Today, it's questions about stem cell research and abortion. It's what to do with the little boy with autism who's disrupting Sunday School, or the marriage that's cracking apart from caring 24/7 for a parent with Alzheimer's. It's about violence spilling out of our homes and into the streets and trying to live a Christian witness in a self-absorbed society that idolizes money and beauty. And most importantly, it's the church that feels paralyzed to do anything or too uninformed to speak.

You've had it happen to you, too . . .

- You're at a hair salon and the woman next to you makes it clear to everyone within a 15-foot radius that she "can't stand all these right-wing radicals who keep invading people's privacy with their prolife nonsense."
- You're in a hospital cafeteria discussing treatment options for your elderly parent with Parkinson's disease, and the talk turns to stem cell research.
- You've been told by your college professor to give a written and oral opinion on the subject of eugenics and social engineering.
- You watch your nephew with cerebral palsy reach his teens then sink into depression because he realizes he may never drive or date.
- A family in your community wants to "pull the plug" on their disabled daughter who hasn't moved or spoken or fed herself in 10 years.
- You are trying to teach Sunday School but are ready to throw in the towel because little Bobby who has autism scares the other children with his shrieking.

- Your uncle has terminal cancer and wants to move to a state where physician-assisted suicide is legal.
- A couple at your church had been approached by an in-vitro clinic that can help them select the sex of their next child.

When *you* have been asked for your opinion, what do you say? How do you respond to your coworkers, classmates, relatives or coffee-klatch friends like Shirley? Whether they are skeptics, cynics or just fellow Christians looking for a little help, the Bible constantly exhorts us to be ready to give a biblical perspective to those who ask (see Prov. 31:9; 1 Pet. 3:15).

Never have we been so bombarded with such sticky ethical dilemmas. These moral problems aren't discussed in dry abstract theory; they are often haggled out in emotional counseling sessions or parking lot arguments after church. They surface when a teenager suffers a life-altering accident and decides to leave a suicide note. Or when a pastor and the parents of a child with a disability dicker over how to include—really include—the family. Life's tough issues often catch us off guard—like when we're just having coffee with a friend. And we need help. We need wisdom and guidance.

My Personal Journey

As a result of a 1967 diving accident that left me a quadriplegic, I was pushed up against a wall of questions, some of them similar to Shirley's. Relegated to the geriatric ward of a state institution for nearly two years (the doctors didn't know what to do with young spinal-cord injured people like me), I fell into depression. When I was told I would never walk again or use my hands, the depression turned into despair. I didn't want to live in a wheel-chair paralyzed for the rest of my life; I wanted to die! I would beg my high school friends to help me end my life: "Why won't you bring in your father's razors or your mother's sleeping pills? Can't you see the misery I'm in?"

Thankfully, God placed people around me who weren't afraid of my questions; they helped me get to the bottom of my despair and discouragement. I remember asking one Christian friend named Steve, "Surely God understands how hard it is to be a quadriplegic. I know I'm going to heaven anyway, so show me in the Bible where it's wrong to arrange an 'early exit.'" The look on Steve's face was sheer terror. I don't think anyone had ever con-fronted him with such a tough issue—I was asking him if mercy killing is okay when the suffering is too much to bear. He was honest enough to tell me that he didn't know the answer but would get back to me. The next day he did. He flipped to Exodus 20:13 and read, "You shall not murder." He closed his Bible, and then said softly, but sincerely, "And, Joni, I think your conscience will tell you that includes 'self-murder.'"

That simple answer didn't suddenly turn me around, but it was one in a series of milestones that led me to pray, "Then, God, if I can't die, please show me how to live." It didn't happen over-night, but slowly I began to embrace God's purposes in my life, even if it meant total and permanent paralysis.

Of all the things I learned in the ensuing years, one phrase still resonates. Before Steve left for Bible college, he told me, "Don't ever forget, Joni, God permits what He hates to accom-plish what He loves." It's true. God permitted what He hated (a cruel cross) to accomplish that which He prized (glorifying His

mercy and winning our salvation). I discovered the same principle applied to me. God permitted what He despised—my wheelchair—to accomplish something that He loved—my character
honed, my faith refined and my hope in Christ cemented. It's the
same principle underscored in 1 Peter 2:21: "To this you were
called, because Christ suffered for you, leaving you an example,
that you should follow in his steps."

I didn't necessarily receive all my answers, but the hard questions didn't seem to matter as much. As I delighted myself in the
Lord, He gave me the desire of my heart—not miraculous healing,
but a sweeter, more intimate union with Jesus Christ (see Ps. 37:4).

Learning to Speak Up

You might be wondering how an author and an artist in a wheelchair like me got involved in ethical issues in the public arena. I
never much cared for the social sciences when I was in school;
during my time at the University of Maryland, I chose classes in
art appreciation and English literature. It was during that same
time—around the early '70s—that I began sharing my story at local churches in Baltimore where I lived. Having learned how to
paint holding a brush between my teeth (remember, I'm a quadriplegic), I began exhibiting my drawings at art fairs during the
summers. That led to a Baltimore TV interview or two (with
Oprah Winfrey, no less, before she moved and made it big in
Chicago). After that, Barbara Walters asked me to appear on *The
Today Show* in 1974. A publisher was inspired by the interview,
and I was asked to write a book. In 1976, the *Joni* book hit the
shelves as well as the *New York Times'* international best-seller list.

Shortly after that, the film division of the Billy Graham Evangelistic Association decided to make a movie of my life.

Did I ever begin receiving letters! Many letters were from readers of *Joni* who simply wrote to tell me they were inspired by my story and wanted to purchase a print of my artwork. But other letters were different—very different. Some were letters from quadriplegics like me who were still depressed from living so long under a thick cloud of despair. Some were from pastors, who were wondering how to help people like me in their churches. Other letters were from parents of children with disabilities; they were wondering how I developed such a positive self-image as a teenager when I couldn't walk or use my hands. Other letters were darker. They were more like suicide notes.

I didn't realize it back then, but God used these hard questions to prepare me for something bigger. I sensed God calling me to share the help and hope I had found in His Word with a widening world of hurting families. When I realized the insights I had gleaned from my personal Bible studies would be tested on others—many of them in situations more desperate than mine—I knew I had to dig deeper.

At first, I felt overwhelmed. In college my attitude was "Don't give me the *War and Peace* version. Cut to the bottom line; just answer my questions." Systems of morality? Absolute truth? Wasn't right and wrong as easy to discern as black and white? Moralistic codes were of little use to me. Just state the plain facts: Was it right or wrong? Just tell me. Too often I refused to take the time or mental energy to dig through the issues.

I may be describing you. You may agree that it's easier to take a casual approach. Usually, we skirt along the edges of an ethical issue, catching an occasional idea or two, or we get a buzz from someone else's turn of phrase. Or perhaps it's not a lazy mental attitude at all. Maybe we're fearful. If we start speaking out on these issues, our neighbors and coworkers might think badly of us. But we've got to get over what the Bible calls a fear of man. If we're nervous about what the Bible really *does* say about today's tough issues, we cannot cave into that fear; we can't afford to worry about what others think of us. I was discussing this with a friend; he observed, "Courage is merely choosing between your fears."[1] We should be more afraid of the judgment of God on us for *not* speaking up, than we are of people's reproach!

In this "brave new world," which Aldous Huxley described in his futuristic novel *Brave New World,* Christians can no longer afford to be bystanders in the public debate. The health of our communities and our families is at stake. The chance for the church to be a force for change in our society is on the line. We need to understand God's heart in these matters and His wisdom, the kind of wisdom described in James 1:5-6: "If, in the process, any of you does not know how to meet any *particular problem* he has only to ask God . . . and he may be quite sure that the *necessary wisdom* will be given him. But he must ask in sincere faith without any secret doubts" (*Phillips*, emphasis added).

Right there, God supplies the answer to how to be a good ambassador for Him in a high-tech society that has discarded the Judeo-Christian ethic. God promises He will give wisdom—that is, the power to discern the soundest response and course of action based on knowledge and experience. God gives hand-tailored wisdom for every discussion—in a classroom, in a hospital waiting room, on an ethics committee, over dinner with Christians or having coffee with a neighbor. And His custom-fitted wisdom is needed for discerning how to live a balanced life in our topsy-turvy society.

So let's not be timid about exercising mental muscle as we study today's tough ethical issues. And let's not be fearful of the answers we find—answers that are accompanied by a commensurate responsibility to tell others (see Eph. 4:15; 5:11-13). Let's be prepared to dig for God's wisdom in order to be His light in a confused and conflicted world.

> My son, if you accept my words and store up my commands within you, turning your ear to wisdom and applying your heart to understanding, and if you call out for insight and cry aloud for understanding, and if you look for it as for silver and search for it as for hidden treasure, then you will understand the fear of the LORD and find the knowledge of God (Prov. 2:1-5).

The Tough Issues . . . What Are They?

During my years at Joni and Friends, I've met amazing people—most of them, like me, have looked hard into the Bible for guidance after a tragic accident or a devastating illness. Spending time with them has inspired me. Watching the way they've handled the tough issues in their lives has driven me even deeper into the Word of God.

You will be introduced to some of these inspiring people in *Life in the Balance*. When Joni and Friends produced television episodes highlighting their stories in our TV series, we realized their life examples would perfectly illustrate the tough questions covered in *Life in the Balance*. And, oh, has God used the stories of these people to help others gain a biblical worldview on everything from abortion to autism . . . from euthanasia to eugenics . . . from genocide to a new generation absorbed with "self"!

This is why I'm so excited you're holding *Life in the Balance* in your hands. You can now begin to grapple with and better understand these issues through these chapters and through the Bible studies and DVD clips of peoples' stories found in the *Life in the Balance Leader's Guide*. This book is full of practical wisdom for every believer who is looking for that reason, that good word of defense, that unique way of articulating a Christian perspective on stem cell research, violence in the streets, modern genocide, and much more.

So let me introduce you to the specific topics we'll be covering and give you an overview of the content and the inspiring people you will meet on the DVD.

When Life Isn't Fair: Violence in the Streets

Perhaps the most important issue to tackle first is this issue of fairness. Fundamentally, we want life to be fair. We want people to treat us fairly. We want God to treat us with fairness. When this doesn't happen, we feel angry and cheated. *God's not fair,* we fume, and we begin to think of Him as untrustworthy. We view Him as a threatened, pacing deity, starving for affection and with His finger on the nuclear button. Such a rebellious and self-centered orientation toward God can't help but unlock the floodgates of all sorts of personal and societal ills. When things *don't* go our way, then we feel violated. That violation breeds anger. And anger unchecked begets violence.

My friend Vicky Olivas has experienced firsthand what happens in a society where violence is almost a way of life—anger and violence in the schoolyard, the workplace, on the freeway and on the street. She was in the middle of a job interview when her prospective employer lured her into a warehouse—Vicky ended up being shot during an attempted rape. If anyone had a right to accuse God of being unfair, it was her. Instead, Vicky's story serves as a perfect illustration of how God is with us in the dark places of our lives and leads us into His glorious light.

Making Sense of Autism

Once, while scheduled to speak at a well-known Christian college, I was hosted by Greg and Marla during my stay. I had the pleasure of getting to know their children, one of whom, Christian, had autism. On the last night of my visit, I asked Greg if we could take his family out to dinner. He seemed a little hesitant, but then gathered the family and met us at the local Red Lobster restaurant. It was a Friday night, and the place was crowded. I noticed that Christian was very fidgety; his daddy was trying everything to keep Christian entertained. When we were finally seated, this little boy simply had had enough noise and confusion—Christian went ballistic. I will never forget the expressions of embarrassment on the faces of Greg and Marla. And I will never forget the disapproving stares and whispers from the other diners. It was my first up-close experience of what families with children with autism must face every day.

Of all the disabilities on the scene, autism is arguably the most prevalent, yet the least understood. Just ask any parent of a child with autism. When such a child is born into the family, mom and dad must suddenly become experts, searching for treatment and therapy, a school that will embrace their child, and a church that will do the same.

You would hope that the church would be a model of compassion and acceptance, but that's not always the case. Pat Verbal is Manager of Curriculum Development at the Christian Institute on Disability at Joni and Friends. She has served as a Christian education specialist for more than 20 years and knows how ill-equipped and unprepared church leaders are to handle a child whose behavior is often erratic and explosive. In this chapter, Pat helps us understand how to include children who the Bible says are indispensable to the church. She unveils four hidden truths about autism that will open your heart to the struggles and cries for help from families like Greg and Marla's.

Self-Image in a Fickle Culture

Ours is a world that idolizes beauty and brains. In our quick-fix, no-deposit-no-return culture, is there room for broken and marginalized people? Consider my friend Holly Strother. Hers is a face that could easily be chosen for the cover of *Seventeen Magazine*. With large dark eyes, thick black hair and a full and ready smile, Holly is truly a beautiful young woman. She's also been blessed with a sharp intellect—Holly recently completed her master's degree in sociology and serves the mentally and emotionally ill community.

But for all her beauty and brains, Holly's life is not easy. She struggles to keep her head high in a world that, for the most part, has no time or room for wheelchair users—Holly has spina bifida, is very short for her age, walks with crutches and occasionally must use a wheelchair. Although she possesses a winsome personality, making friends in a "stand up" world can be a challenge. Yes, she's got great looks, but Holly has yet to have a serious relationship with a young man. Friday nights can sometimes feel long and lonely.

Women aren't the only ones in a conundrum in an *American Idol* society. How many young men do you know who are in need of a healthy self-image? Sure, many say they're okay, but stripped of their Facebook, iPhone, ability to play sports, their cool clothes, their hot cars and their friends, young men feel emotionally naked and extremely vulnerable. These teens and young adults need to get reoriented in biblical values and time-less principles of self-worth.

For all of Holly's talent and beauty, she has worked hard to ground her self-image in things far deeper than the latest shade of nail color. Her entire character is totally oriented toward God and the value He places on her life. This alone has given my friend a consummate poise and dignity that throws shadows on any runway model. And we can learn many lessons from Holly. Through Holly's story, you'll be equipped to guide the young people you know through the clamor of societal voices to a quiet and calm dignity that can only be found in understanding what it truly *means* to be created in the image of a God who cares.

Searching for the Greater Good: The Stem Cell Debate

As a survivor of a spinal cord injury, I am intensely interested in research that will lead to a cure. My husband, Ken, and I sup-port spinal cord injury research. We are constantly keeping abreast of the latest findings that, we hope, will one day cure paralysis—if not for someone with a chronic injury like mine, then for people whose spinal injury is new. We are convinced that one day there *will* be a cure!

That cure probably will come out of stem cell research. If cures are within reach, why are so many people debating the ethics of stem cell research? People on both sides of the debate agree that we need to find cures for diseases such as Alzheimer's and Parkinson's. Both sides have compassion for those suffering from life-threatening cancers and serious injuries. We both agree that federal funding of research to find cures is necessary. But we disagree on which *kind* of stem cell research to pursue.

Stem cells are the body's master cells; that is, they are blank-slate cells that are very flexible, pliable and have the miraculous ability to transform into almost any other kind of body tissue. The body manufactures its own stem cells in places like bone marrow, nasal tissue, dental pulp, certain fatty areas and blood. There are even stem cells in umbilical cord blood that seem to have special properties in morphing into other tissue.

However, stem cells are also found in human embryos. Some researchers are convinced that these stem cells have much more flexibility and pliability and, therefore, are able to be nurtured into many more other kinds of tissue. However—and this is the rub of the debate—researchers have to kill the human embryo in order to harvest its stem cells.

So the question is, is destroying one life in order to cure another morally right? In this hotly emotional debate, there *is* reason and sanity. And there are commonsense answers. So in chapter 5, on stem cell issues, you will become equipped to understand both sides of the ethical argument and be able to judge for yourself what is morally objectionable and what is not.

The Truth Behind the Pain of Abortion
Look up the word "abortion" in the dictionary and you'll most likely read: "Also called voluntary abortion; the removal of an em-

bryo or fetus from the uterus in order to end a pregnancy."[2] The dictionary definition makes abortion sound almost sterile and acceptable. However, the surgical dismemberment of an unborn child is anything but clean and clinical. And that's partly why this is such a *tough* issue—it involves the murder of millions of human beings.

Murder? You may be thinking, *Joni, isn't your language a little inflammatory?* The abortion of an unborn child is the most fundamental violation of that child's rights—the right to life. And the abortion debate largely centers on the contest of personal rights—either the right of the woman to choose, or the right of the child to live.

Do not be uneasy about the word "rights." When the Bible speaks of rights, as it does in Proverbs 31:8, it means *moral claims* that can be made on society—claims that can be backed up by the law. Notice they are *moral* claims; true rights have their basis in God's moral law. But cut loose from the Bible, rights become merely people's willful determinations dressed up in politically correct language in order to give them a showy kind of dignity or respectability.[3] And then, the exercise of rights becomes nothing more than a national competition between who's more victimized than whom. We become a haranguing group of competing individuals who are no longer interested in the common good. When that happens, the first to be impacted are the weak, the vulnerable and the unborn—and it all began back in 1973, in the *Roe v. Wade* Supreme Court decision, which ruled that the right to privacy was inherent in the U.S. Constitution; that, in turn, protected a woman's right to have an abortion.

This fateful court decision has not only brought suffering and death to the unborn, but it also continues to devastate millions of women who struggle with the horrible guilt and shame of having aborted a human life. In this chapter, you'll hear about Sheila Harper's journey from the pain of abortion to forgiveness and peace. Sheila is the founder of SaveOne, a ministry that reaches out to women and men suffering in silence after an abortion. You'll meet Nancy and David Guthrie, who chose to ignore their *legal right* to an abortion and found a priceless treasure in their daughter Hope.

A Calloused Conscience: Eugenics and Genocide
When we hear the word "genocide," we usually think of the gas ovens of Auschwitz, the pogroms of Stalin or the near annihilation of the Armenian people by the Turks. We may even think of more recent examples of ethnic cleansing in Cambodia or in Bosnia. But there's a more subtle kind of genocide that doesn't always grab the headlines or the attention of the evening news.

Back in the '80s, I was appointed to the National Council on Disability under Presidents Reagan and Bush. During my tenure, our 15-member council reviewed scores of government reports relating to disability. One of them was a preliminary report submitted by the National Institutes of Health in Washington, DC. Under the heading of "Disability Prevention," the NIH was considering the merits of abortion as a kind of disability prevention strategy. In other words, disabilities such as Down syndrome or spina bifida could be prevented by encouraging more mothers carrying unborn children with these conditions to abort. All 15 members of our council were shocked by the suggestion (it's interesting that our council was a mix of Republicans and Democrats)! We wasted no time in sending the report back to the National Institutes of Health for revision.

Oh, what different times we live in now! Now, the American College of Obstetricians and Gynecologists recommends offering Down syndrome screening to all pregnant women. Susan Enouen of Physicians for Life states, "If current trends continue, it may eventually become 'unacceptable' for parents to continue a pregnancy knowing that their baby has Down syndrome. Recent U.S. studies have indicated that when Down syndrome is diagnosed prenatally, 84% to 91% of those babies will be killed by abortion."[4]

This is a more subtle and pervasive kind of genocide than the sort we saw in Armenia or Europe during World War II. It's a modern-day effort to socially engineer a more "acceptable" society through the eradication of certain disabling conditions. Trouble is, when you remove the condition, you can remove the person *with* the condition. It dare not happen to my friend Robin Hiser.

Robin is a woman with Down syndrome who serves on the leadership team at one of our Joni and Friends' Family Retreats. She has a passion for Jesus Christ and a deep desire to give Christian compassion to other people like her. As Robin often says, "Worship of God is in my blood!" Her story gives an actual face to the tough issue of eugenics. I can't imagine how poor our world would be without people like her.

From Obscurity to Celebrity by Way of Tragedy: End-of-Life Issues
Those who are weak and infirmed—the elderly and medically fragile—have never fared well in societies that have lost their moral center. Look what happened a little more than 60 years ago in Nazi Germany. Those with mental and physical handicaps were the first to be carted away in the dark from institutions. But they were not just *any* disabled people. Nazi medical teams singled out

disabled people in institutions who had no visitors, no family members, no advocates or friends to speak up for them. No one cared to speak up for these individuals' most basic right—the right to life.

Now, just decades later, Dr. Peter Singer, professor of bioethics at Princeton University, insists that those with profound mental retardation, people in comas or individuals living with Alzheimer's disease have no rights; they have no voice; they need no advocacy. He attests that people who lack rational capabilities—who lack self-awareness—have no personhood; they need no advocacy because they have no rights.[5] So what if an infant with Down syndrome was starved to death? Many intellectuals in the bioethical debate would call him a pre-person. An individual in a coma might be labeled a nonperson.

I am *amazed* how quickly this view has saturated thinking in our society. A utilitarian view emphasizes one's usefulness, and once society begins assessing life worth based on a person's functioning ability or usefulness, those who are too weak, too old or too disabled can be targeted. People are being treated as *things,* not individuals with inherent worth and human dignity. Society says that it treats its people with dignity, but it does not; it *cannot.* Once you take God out of the picture, people are only "glorified animals." People have no value, because most people in our society no longer believe we are *created* or *made in the image of God.*

This life view impacts every level of our society—medicine, education, politics, as well as the allocation of resources. Our culture has no real room for those who are weak and infirmed; no room for people who strain Medicare or who drain the grandkids' college fund or who contribute nothing more to society than medical bills. Society views suffering with contempt and disdain—we want to avoid it, escape or eradicate it or do away with it. Sadly, it is then only a short philosophical jump to the point where we begin to treat people who suffer with disdain and contempt. And it is not just the elderly, newborn, unborn or the disabled who are at risk—are not the lives of all of us jeopardized when life can be starved, altered and aborted, cloned, copied, euthanized or eradicated?

In this book, we will examine the value of life and the dangers of utilitarianism in "From Obscurity to Celebrity by Way of Tragedy: End-of-Life Issues." Terri Schiavo is the young brain-injured woman who was denied a feeding tube by court order, depriving her of her right to live. That single court decision opened a Pandora's box that has impacted the lives of countless people in comas or with serious brain injuries.

I've Got Questions About the American Dream

America has always touted a rugged brand of individualism. The Bill of Rights guarantees us the right to life, liberty and the pursuit of happiness. But our Founding Fathers recognized that this pursuit needed to be balanced with moral restraint. In fact, one of the most referenced parts of George Washington's farewell address was his strong support of the importance of religion and morality in American life. Washington went so far as to say that the nation's morality cannot be maintained without religion.[6]

In the twenty-first century, however, America has a new religion—its own radical individualism that lacks the checks and balances of Christian principles. Without the restraints of moral prudence, people feel free to pursue their own individual desires with abandon; and that, in turn, can breed materialism and greed. This is often to the detriment of others, such as we saw on Wall Street in 2008, in the near collapse of the U.S. banking system, which included a pandemic of home foreclosures and job losses.

We can't seem to cope without adding the latest and newest application onto our Blackberry or Droid or iPhone. We simply must have that pair of Jimmy Choo shoes on sale at Nordstrom for $350. Even Wal-Mart shoppers can become consumed—when you shop, shop, shop for that bargain until you nearly drop, something's a little out of balance. Materialism refers to how a person or group chooses to spend their money and time. Literally, a materialist is a person for whom collecting material goods is an important priority.[7] We are driven by the goal of perfection—having the perfect 4G network device; an entertainment system in our cars and homes; the perfect job in which we feel happy and productive; and even the perfect sleep system (they no longer call them mattresses). No wonder the latest trend among many American families is to rent their own Public Storage unit—it's what happens when your garage overflows with "stuff."

This is why it's so refreshing to be around someone for whom accumulating "stuff" is just not his thing. I'm thinking of my friend Nick Vujicic, who has a worldwide ministry speaking to millions of people around the globe. He was born without arms and legs, yet Nick does not let that slow him down. Piling up things in his home, garage and driveway isn't his focus. Nick has been forced by God to limit his options of temptation—that's what happens when you can't drive a car, fit into Armani jackets or play Wii.

As an able-bodied man with a young family, and living in trendy Southern California, Steve Bundy is inspired by Nick's life of faith. Steve, like Nick, has been caught up in the "if only" syndrome. "If only" we lived in a bigger house or "if only" I had a better car, and so on. We've all been there. In this chapter, Steve challenges us to embrace God's economic system and teach our families to value what He values.

Let's Get Started!

I hope that now you can see why I am so excited about this book, *Life in the Balance*. It's my prayer that as you and your family or small group work through this study, God will "equip you with everything good for doing his will, and may he work in us what is pleasing to him, through Jesus Christ, to whom be glory forever and ever. Amen" (Heb. 13:21). Together may we be shining witnesses of what it means to live as God intended people to live—and may our testimonies convict and convince a dark and hurting world of the truth of God and His Word. It's what happens when we live *Life in the Balance!*

> *God, we confess that many of these issues are beyond*
> *our comprehension. We need Your Spirit to open our understanding.*
> *Show us Your truth that we might act according to Your will,*
> *to seek balance in our own lives and*
> *to offer hope to others through Jesus Christ our Lord.*
> *Amen.*

STUDY QUESTIONS

1. Where do you turn to get the news? How do you interpret what you read or watch?

2. Has anyone ever asked you what you believe about one of these issues?

   - Violence
   - Genocide
   - Life Worth
   - Materialism
   - Abortion
   - Autism
   - Self-Image
   - Stem Cell Research

3. Rate the topics in this book using the following scale:

   (1) I don't think much about it.
   (2) It is somewhat important to me.
   (3) I know people who are coping with it.
   (4) It keeps me awake at night.

4. Do you believe that God's Word provides truth and answers to all of these questions?

5. Even the lives of followers of Christ can get out of balance at times. How do you handle this when it happens?

6. Steve told Joni, "God permits what He hates to accomplish what He loves." Have you ever witnessed a time when this happened to someone?

7. How would you define an ethical dilemma?

8. How are our culture's ethical debates putting the health of our communities and families at risk?

9. How can the Church be a force for change when our society is at stake?

2

When Life Isn't Fair: Violence in the Streets

By Joni Eareckson Tada

Shocking headlines often miss the real stories. Take this 1997 caption: "Ennis Cosby Murdered on LA Freeway 405." People assumed the son of Hollywood royalty might have gotten into drugs or the dangerous behaviors common for children of celebrities. The truth was that Ennis was by all reports a wonderful young man who had overcome dyslexia to graduate from Morehouse College and was attending Columbia University to become a special education teacher. He spent his last afternoon on earth tutoring children with learning disabilities. Mikhail Markhasev was convicted of the shooting, and sentenced to life without parole. Markhasev initially appealed the verdict, but he dropped his appeal in 2001, writing in a letter to the attorney general: "I am guilty, and I want to do the right thing. . . . More than anything, I want to apologize to the victim's family. It is my duty as a Christian, and it's the least I can do, after the great wickedness for which I am responsible."[1]

> *The LORD is my light and my salvation—*
> *whom shall I fear?*
> *The LORD is the stronghold of my life—*
> *of whom shall I be afraid?*
>
> Psalm 27:1

Chicago Kids Too Scared to Leave Home
Chicago Sun Times, August 6, 2008

"I can't go outside"—Many Chicago kids are scared to go to the store. Others avoid stepping off their block or going to the park; they've lost the freedom to play. Eleven-year-old Maria Rivera is afraid to play in front of her own home. She spends much of her free time indoors, alone with her mom. Fear of the guns and gangs that plague her Little Village neighborhood has left Maria virtually a prisoner in her own home.[2]

The first time I saw Vicky Olivas, she was sitting in her wheelchair in the corner of the physical therapy lab, her paralyzed hands propped on a lap pillow. Although Latin and lovely looking, she seemed to prefer being by herself. Intrigued, I asked one of the physical therapists about her. "Vicky's only been paralyzed a few years," he offered. "She's really had a rough time." I quickly learned just how rough.

It was 1976 when Vicky's husband walked out on her and their two-year-old son, Arturo. For the first time in her life, Vicky was faced with the challenge of finding a job to support herself and her little boy. *Can I even do this?* she thought, as she stood in front of the hallway mirror, deciding what to wear for a job interview.

It wasn't easy. A woman from the employment agency called on a Friday afternoon: "I have a lead for you, but the employer wants to see you right away. It's an interview you shouldn't miss."

It was an inconvenient time and it meant borrowing money for gas. Nevertheless, she decided to go.

The address in the industrial park was hard to find. When she located the building, she parked at the curb and looked down a long alley. Vicky hesitated. By now it was late afternoon, and the area looked a little run down. *Well,* she thought, *I've come this far. I may as well go through with the interview.* She walked down the alley to the last door of a warehouse. You know that feeling—the one when the hairs on the back of your neck stand up? You're not sure why, but you sense pending danger.

Vicky stepped into the office, but no one was there. The floor was strewn with paper, and the place had a damp, closed-in smell. She peeked around the corner and called, "Hello? Is anyone here?" She walked through the warehouse and found a side room where two men were sitting—one behind a desk and the other slouched in a plastic chair with his arms folded. "My name is Vicky Olivas. The employment agency sent me over."

The man behind the desk—obviously the boss—leaned back and looked her up and down. "Yes, I've been expecting you," he said. "Do you have a résumé?"

"No," she said, "not with me."

He slid an application across the desk and ordered, "Here. Go back to the reception area and fill it out while I finish here." Resigned to seeing the interview through, Vicky began filling in the information. She glanced toward the open warehouse and noticed two men unloading boxes from a truck. By the time they finished and pulled away, she had completed the form. That's when the owner entered the room and closed the door behind him. He clicked the lock and a chill went down Vicky's spine.

"Let's go into my office," he said, motioning toward another part of the building.

That's when the nightmare started. Suddenly the man grabbed her from behind and threw her against the wall. "Do you realize this was all planned?" he whispered hoarsely. "I asked them to send somebody just like you. I've sent everyone else home. It's just us here." He clutched at Vicky's blouse, while she struggled with all her might to push him away. Out of the corner of her eye she spotted metal. A gun! She wrestled harder to free herself.

Suddenly . . . *bang!*

The room spiraled as Vicky slumped to the floor. Her thoughts spun out of control as he dragged her limp body down the hallway. *This can't be happening! Where is he taking me?* He pulled her into a small room and her face flopped against cold, smelly tiles—he had dumped her in a bathroom! Blood began to pool around her face. She strained to lift her arms, but they didn't respond. The man left, but in a few moments returned. He wiped his brow and kept repeating in a shaky voice, "I didn't mean to shoot you! I didn't mean to do it!"

The odor of the filthy bathroom made Vicky's head spin. Everything became blurry, but she was able to sense someone else entering the room. It was a woman, and she started yelling, "What have you done? Now what are we going to do?!"

The next thing Vicky knew, they had thrown her into a car and were racing her to a nearby hospital. They quickly handed Vicky over to the emergency room attendants, who rushed her inside. With that, the car sped off. When Vicky saw several policemen inside the emergency room, she finally felt safe. As doctors assessed Vicky's injury, she told a policewoman her horrific story.

But, sadly, no one believed her. That is, until the police went back to the warehouse and found her purse, a trail of blood, and a gun in the trash pail. They were able to trace the description of the car and within hours had captured her assailant.

It's a sad story, but the ending has an even sadder twist. The attacker, who had three other convictions of attempted rape, was released after only three years in jail. Vicky, on the other hand, will spend the rest of her life in a wheelchair completely paralyzed from the neck down.

Have you faced a situation where your worst fears actually came true? Most of us will never be attacked as Vicki was, but the Bible says that we will be tested.

A Culture of Violence

Vicky's story would test the faith of the most steadfast saint. It nearly ruined what little faith she had! For many months, and through painful hours of rehabilitation, Vicky fought to hold depression at bay. Through the compassionate support of several Christian friends, it was amazing that she was ultimately able to seek out the God of the Bible and place her trust in Him. As she told me years later when I met her, "I have nowhere else to go but up. And I'm tired of feeling sorry for myself. I know I'll only get stronger if I put my faith in Jesus." And that is exactly what she did. The change in her life was obvious by the way she studied the Bible and quickly grew in the Lord.

But one question kept nagging her: Why should her attacker get off easy while she had to face a life sentence of paralysis in a wheelchair? She dove deeper into God's Word, but she kept stumbling across verses like "consider it pure joy" (Jas. 1:2) when you face trials. The Bible seemed to be telling her to snap out of it and just learn to rejoice in suffering (see Rom. 5:3). Then, like rubbing salt into a wound, she was expected to forgive that wicked man!

You don't have to be a quadriplegic to understand Vicky's frustrations. Fundamentally, we want life to be fair. We want people to treat us fairly. But life is not wired that way. Jesus was right when He said, "In this world you will have trouble" (John 16:33). His words sound like more of a promise than just a reality check!

Often the "trouble" Jesus warns of comes at the hands of other people over whom we have no control . . . people who have been raised in and conditioned by a society filled with violence . . . people who care nothing about bridling their passions and who have no resources to deal with anger . . . people for whom civility and behavioral restraint are foreign concepts. Just consider these stunning statistics:

- Every two minutes, someone in the United States is sexually assaulted.[3]
- There are more than 1 million gang members in the United States.[4]
- Almost 5 children die every day as a result of child abuse.[5]
- Half of the 3.5 million violent crimes in families are committed against a spouse.[6]
- Between 1 and 2 million American seniors have been injured or exploited by someone on whom they depended for protection.[7]
- In 2006, more than one-third of serious violent crimes perpetrated against youth (ages 12-18) took place at or on the way to school.[8]

• People with developmental disabilities are 6 times more likely to be victims of crime than other people are.[9]

When we read statistics like these, we tend to think such violence happens only to other people, not to us or to our families. When Vicky set out on her job interview, she never dreamed it would end so horribly. But no one is immune. Perhaps *you* have experienced great harm or injury at the hands of a relative . . . or your spouse . . . a neighbor . . . or even a stranger. Violence has become an ugly cancer in our culture. Some people insist its rise is fostered by the disintegration of the family unit. Others point to violent movies and video games or the growing disregard for civil law. Some even say it's bred into the American mindset of radical individualism. Little wonder it's a subject under so much intense scrutiny by sociologists and psychologists.

What is clear is that violence—and the anger that foments it—is escalating. Politicians, news magazines and talk-show hosts are making earnest appeals for a climate of civility. There are even television ads urging people to behave politely and treat one another with respect. People in the United States seem to be nervously aware that our national anger is a symptom of a disintegrating society.

There is no disagreement that civilized people want a more respectful society, but can it be achieved by education and awareness-raising only? How do we collectively put a lid on so much societal rage? Is it a matter of more and better law enforcement? Community classes for prospective parents? Censoring violent movies? Preventing game manufacturers from producing video games filled with blood and guns? Although most people who exhibit violent behavior were the victims of violence themselves when they were young, is the only answer to remove more children from abusive homes?[10]

How do we reverse the trend? How can we exorcise the violent tendencies that reside within the human heart?

What Exactly Is Anger?

Have you ever been boiling mad? Then welcome to the human race. It's curious how we treat anger as if it's an emotional fluid inside of us that builds up pressure. When we get angry, we can almost picture our resentment rising like hot steam inside a pressure cooker. We even say that people are *filled* with anger or are *ready to explode*. We think of anger as something inside of us that is *pent-up,* and every once in a while we have to *blow off steam* or *get it off our chests*. And when our anger is *spent* or *released* . . . ah . . . we just feel better. All these metaphors depict anger as a kind of pressurized substance inside of us.

My friend David Powlison of the Christian Counseling Education Foundation describes this as the "hydraulic" way of looking at anger. In his booklet *Anger: Escaping the Maze,* David writes, "There's no doubt that these colorful descriptions *do* capture how anger feels, but they don't define what anger *is*. But when we believe that anger is something inside of us—rather than something we actually *do*—then we cannot effectively deal with it."[11] David Powlison knows counselors who have told people, "Take a baseball bat and wallop a pillow; it's a harmless, constructive way of getting anger out of your system. Believe me, you'll feel all the better for it." Well, you won't.

That's because anger is a moral act. Some anger, however, is understandable. When a person has suffered great loss, anger is a "natural" part of the grief process—in this respect, anger is logical. At the same time, anger caused by grief is still a truthful expression of your character. Anger is not a thing inside of you; it is an indication that something is amiss and must be dealt with.

In Ephesians 4:26, Paul states, "In your anger do not sin." Feeling angry is not sinful, but it becomes sinful when we don't surrender that anger to God and choose to act out on our angry feelings. And anger at God, which is frequently revealed in counseling, almost always becomes sinful anger. The core of most anger stems from feeling violated or feeling out of control and is an indication that something needs to be confessed and made right. James 1:19-20 says, "Everyone should be quick to listen, slow to speak and slow to become angry, for man's anger does not bring about the righteous life that God desires."

Vicky Olivas knew that she had been harboring a deep, seething anger against the man who had attempted to rape her. For many months she had been focusing on *his* sin. However, her anger was an expression of the sin of unforgiveness having sway in her *own* life. Her quiet rage wasn't "righteous" in God's eyes, because she was not allowing God's grace and forgiveness to flow through her heart to her attacker (see Matt. 6:14-15; Mark 11:25). This was a humbling concept that was, at first, difficult to grasp.

The Seed of Violence

Ever since Cain erupted in anger against his brother, Abel (see Gen. 4:6), violence has plagued man. If we take a closer look at the story, we see that the root of Cain's anger is inextricably linked to his relationship with God. When God accepted Abel's offering, but not Cain's, resentment grew in Cain's heart. Left unchecked, Cain's resentment turned quickly to violence and murder. Yes, the murder of Abel . . . but down deep, it was also Cain's way of striking out at God.

I can identify with Cain. Not long ago, I was at a hotel in a large city when someone snatched my wallet as I entered the lobby elevator. It wasn't until I arrived at my room that we realized it was stolen out of my handbag hanging on my wheelchair. I figured it must have been the two young men who were walking behind me as I wheeled through the lobby to the elevator—they picked me clean just as the elevator doors closed! Feelings of anger welled up within me. Of course, I was angry at them, but mostly, I was generally angry with the whole situation—which, to me, indicated that my real anger was directed at God. Ultimately, I laid the whole wallet-snatching incident at *His* feet. He could have prevented it, but He didn't. And so, I figured the theft was one of those things that could be classed as His fault.

Given the nature of sin—and the larger issue of violence in our society—anger at God is one of the most logical human reactions. But it's a deadly wickedness. You don't often hear that, even from many Christian counselors. Some people say it's okay to feel angry at God, because He made us with angry emotions. And after all, God *does* do disappointing things, so feel free to vent your anger at Him, because He can absorb it. Besides, you'll be able to forgive God for letting you down.

I don't think so.

Anger at God is almost always sinful—it's usually a muddle of malice and mistrust about who we think He is. But anger at God, handled rightly, presents a wonderful opportunity to understand our own hearts:

- First, when we suffer injustice, God has *not* let us down. Nowhere in the Bible do we find a shred of evidence that the Lord ever betrays us. People may betray us, and the devil may torment us. But God neither betrays nor torments us.

- We deceive ourselves when we think that life should be fair. It's not. And it never will be on this side of eternity. Yet God's Word tells us that His plans are *not* to harm us (or treat us unfairly), but to give us hope and a future (see Jer. 29:11). If we truly believe this, anger at Him will dissolve.

- When we place ourselves on the throne of our heart—a throne reserved for the Lord of the universe—our personal rights become the end-all, be-all. We insist we have the right to be respected . . . to be understood . . . to have life go our way. When we are *not* respected by family or friends, or understood by our coworkers; when things *don't* go our way, then we feel violated. That violation breeds anger. And anger unchecked begets violence.

It all comes down to how we relate to God. When we place Jesus Christ on the throne of our hearts and yield our personal rights to Him, purposing to trust Him for whatever happens, we experience true freedom. It takes the supernatural grace of Almighty God to do that, but it's exactly what He provides! Philippians 2:13 describes how God's grace enables us to do the right thing: "For God is working in you, giving you the desire to obey him and the power to do what pleases him" (*NLT*). When it comes to responding in a godly manner to unfair situations, as well as to hurtful people, God's grace is available and abundant. According to Philippians 2:13, when the Lord gives His grace, He's providing (1) the *desire* to do His will, and (2) the *power* to do His will.

Anger *can* be checked! God's grace gives us both the *desire* to yield our rights to Him and the *power* to trust Him when life seems unfair. But we must be careful not to resist that grace, for Hebrews 12:15 tells us, "See to it that no one misses the grace of God and that no bitter root grows up to cause trouble and defile many." Bitterness only pours more fuel on the fire of anger.

I have learned firsthand the dangers of the bitter spirit. Years of living in a wheelchair have taught me to be quick to reach for the grace of God. He supplies the desire and the power to forgive others. Frankly, I am amazed at how quickly my anger dissipates when I admit my wrongdoing and say, "My attitude was way off, so please forgive me." At that point, I feel anger *drain* away (there we go again using that metaphor; but it accurately describes how we feel, doesn't it)!

The important thing to remember is, when life goes horribly wrong—as it did for Vicky—we don't forgive God for what happened. We take a deep breath and trust Him. But what do we do about those who have offended us? Let's get back to Vicky's story and find out.

A Different Perspective

When we left Vicky Olivas (long after rehab), she had embraced Jesus Christ as her Savior, but she was still struggling with bitterness toward her attacker. All she could think was, *Lord, I will never walk again. I've got a leaky leg-bag and I smell like urine, my back aches, and I'll never again be able to hug my son. Maybe You see all of this achieving a purpose, but all I can think about is that man getting off scot-free.*

If you'll recall, the fact that Vicky's attacker escaped real justice only deepened her anger. Thankfully, that did not deter her from reading her Bible. Yet when she came to Romans 5:3 and read "rejoice in our sufferings," her first thought was, *Sure, God, I'll rejoice the day You make things fair!*

As Vicky continued to study and pray, God began to open her eyes to His perspective. She realized that God's perspective changes everything. His is the perspective of eternity—our human sense of fairness is not meant to be balanced in this life (it is to our benefit that we are not satisfied in a world destined for decay)! When it comes to the unfair treatment we receive at the hands of others, God wants us to look at things from His point of view.

The apostle Paul had this eternal point of view when he said, "For our light and momentary troubles are achieving for us an eternal glory that far outweighs them all" (2 Cor. 4:17). Vicky was to learn that all the trouble she was about to endure in her wheelchair had a purpose. An *eternal* purpose. If she could cultivate a godly response in her suffering, it would have a direct bearing on her capacity for joy, worship and service in heaven. The apostle Peter had this eternal view on problems when he wrote to Christian friends who were being flogged and beaten, "In this you greatly rejoice, though now for a little while you may have had to suffer grief of all kinds of trials" (1 Pet. 1:6).

The eternal perspective separates what is transitory from what is lasting. What is transitory (injustice, unfairness and pain) will not endure. But what is lasting (the eternal weight of glory accrued from that pain and from our willingness to forgive) will remain forever. Everything else—deep disappointment and blatant injustices—no matter how real they seem to us on earth, are inconsequential. Earthly hardships are hardly worth noticing.

This was, at first, a shock to Vicky's sensibilities. But the Bible is not saying that Vicky's sufferings—or yours or mine—are light in themselves; rather, paralysis and earthly injustice only *become* light in contrast to the far greater benefit on the other side of the scale. One day that scale of justice will not only balance, it will be weighted heavily (almost beyond comprehension) to our good and to God's glory. It will mean a new appreciation for His justice—not fairness—but justice. It will mean the final destruction of death, disease and devilish men. It will mean the vindication of God's holy name and the restoration of all things under Christ.

There is something else this heavenly perspective does . . .

Turning Bitterness to Forgiveness

Vicky was able to eventually forgive the man who tried to rape her. She was able to do this because of the eternal perspective she discovered in the Bible—she knew that, in the end, justice would have its day. The justice of God will one day either doom that wicked man dead in his transgressions, or God's justice will release him alive in the righteousness of Christ. If Vicky has her way, it will be the latter rather than the former. Why? Because this remarkable woman now understands that the value of a soul—anyone's soul, even the soul of the man who robbed her of life as she knew it—*far* outweighs the personal disappointment of paralysis.

Please don't think that Vicky's capacity to forgive is impossible or incomprehensible. It's what happens when we grab hold of the grace of God; that is, the *desire* and the *power* to forgive others. Perhaps you have been struggling with bitter thoughts toward a person who has hurt you deeply. Would you like to follow Vicky's example of a forgiving spirit? Consider these important steps that she worked through.[12]

- *Forgiveness involves a positive attitude toward the offense rather than a negative attitude toward the offender.* If our focus remains on the offender, it is difficult to not become bitter. But if we focus in a positive way on the offense, we are better able to look at it from an eternal perspective, as well as see how it aids us in this life. With an eternal point of view, both the offender and the offense fade in importance and our response to our problems becomes the major concern. Vicky began to see that her paralysis not only brought her to a saving knowledge of Jesus Christ, but it was also a significant tool in developing Christlike qualities in her life, such as patience, endurance, self-control and trust in God.

- *Forgiveness views the offender as a tool in God's hands.* Jesus Christ could have become bitter toward those who beat Him and nailed Him to the cross, but He looked at them as carrying out the purpose of God for His life. Because of this, He was able to say, "Father, forgive them; for they know not what they do" (Luke 23:34, *KJV*). When Vicky learned about the sovereignty of God and His control over the affairs of men, she realized that God was the one who ultimately allowed the attack to happen. And if Jesus loved her enough to die for her, surely He was trustworthy when it came to allowing her paralysis to happen.

• *Forgiveness recognizes that bitterness is assuming a right we don't have.* Only God has the right to say, "Vengeance is mine; I will repay" (Rom. 12:19, *KJV*). Bitterness, anger and the violence it breeds are an instinctive means of taking revenge toward the one who has offended us. When Vicky saw that her angry feelings were only hurting her, she quickly relinquished her right to "get revenge."

• *Forgiveness involves cooperating with God for the benefit of others.* Forgiving those who offend us provides the opportunity for God to work in their lives. Although Vicky never had the chance to forgive her assailant face to face, others saw her merciful response and became convinced of the forgiveness that God had toward them in their sins. Her life became a flesh-and-blood example of the overwhelming mercy of God.

It was this quality of mercy that revolutionized the life of Vicky Olivas. The tragic events of that fateful day no longer loomed large in her mind as she meditated on the magnitude of

God's mercy. She focused her emotions on the Lord, not on the man who harmed her. Every time she recited The Lord's Prayer, she would pause when she'd pray, "Forgive us our sins just as we have forgiven those who have sinned against us" (see Matt. 6:12). Basically she was asking the Lord to deal with her in the same manner as she dealt with the sins of her attacker. Given that, Vicky wanted to make certain she harbored no bitterness toward the man who tried to rape her. She could be sure there were no barriers between her and God.

"When I think of the horrible injustice Jesus suffered on His cross because of my sins," Vicky once told me, "then the injustice perpetrated against me seems so minor. And when I consider all the awful things Jesus has forgiven me for, how could I not forgive those who have offended me?"

Creating a Culture of Peace

Whenever I'm having a tough day in my wheelchair and need to be reminded of an eternal perspective, I give my friend Vicky Olivas a call. She is the one who now often counsels me, reminding me, "Joni, fairness isn't the issue. God's justice is. One day He'll make it plain to us. In the meantime, we trust Him. And we pray . . . just like I pray for that man who attacked me."

I think you can see why this godly woman is such a blessing to me and to everyone she meets. Vicky's influence is felt far beyond her circle of friends. The people of her community hold her—and the faith she proclaims—in high regard as they watch the way she has handled the tragedy that robbed her of the use of her body. They understand that her response to violence is truly supernatural. People near and far observe Vicky's life and think, *How great her God must be to inspire such loyalty!* Without a doubt, she is a beautiful expression of Jesus' words, "Your love for one another will prove to the world that you are my disciples" (John 13:35, *NLT*). One by one, people's lives are being touched and their hearts changed by her compelling testimony.

And, friend, it is primarily at *this* level that a culture is healed. When individual hearts are altered, so is the heart of a society. Yes, education and awareness-raising are important and, yes, so are controls on violent behavior in our neighborhoods. But the transformation of a violent society into a peaceful one fundamentally happens on an individual level.

God is looking for people who will demonstrate true Christian love and mercy, one person at a time . . . one neighbor, one classmate, one relative, one coworker at a time. He wants His people to be "salt of the earth" (Matt. 5:13), providing a preserving influence for good in our society. He longs for His followers to be the "light of the world" (Matt. 5:14), convicting and convincing a hostile culture that peace is the better way.

Do not be discouraged at the violence you see in your home . . . in your school . . . at your workplace . . . on the freeway. And do not assume the problem is too overwhelming for you to make a difference. Remember the story of my friend Vicky Olivas. She is one woman who is helping to change her community through her Christian witness. Look at her life and draw encouragement, for you, too, are the salt of the earth. You are the light of the world. Take courage from the words of your Savior: "Blessed are the peacemakers, for they will be called children of God" (Matt 5:9, *NRSV*).

It's God's strategy to quench the anger and reclaim this society, this nation, this world as rightfully His.

God, we lift to You all those who have suffered
due to acts of violence. May they find grace and peace.
We pray for people who have committed violent acts.
May they find help and forgiveness. We praise You for men
and women who give their lives to protect others.
May they put their trust in You for protection.
Amen.

STUDY QUESTIONS

1. When you think of violent crimes, what top news stories come to mind?

2. How do these stories make you feel?

3. Have you ever been angry with God? How did you work through your anger?

4. How should we handle anger toward someone who has hurt us?

5. What are the characteristics of a person who is harboring bitterness?

6. Can you see any positives results from your sufferings? If not, can you still trust God that eternity will outweigh your sufferings? Why or why not?

7. Is there someone you don't want to forgive? How does forgiveness for this person now look in light of God's Word?

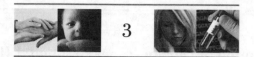

3

Making Sense of Autism

By Pat Verbal

We often hear from pastors who say, "Parents bring children with autism to our church, and we don't know what to do with them!" We also hear from parents who say, "In society, we face fear and isolation because our children have autism. But when we go to church and feel rejected, it hurts even more." In this chapter, you'll meet families who are bravely navigating the complicated world of autism. Their frustrations and tender joys may surprise you, as well as their total dependence on God. You'll discover that families affected by autism don't always want to be on the receiving end. They have a lot to offer. In fact, God tells us that our churches will never be complete without them.

—Joni Eareckson Tada

In the early 1970s, I attended a church in St. Louis, where I volunteered in the children's ministry. Our director called me one Saturday to discuss a new family who would be visiting our Sunday service. She didn't know much about their eight-year-old son, John, except that he couldn't be in class with other children. I quickly offered to stay with John in a separate room. As I gathered Bible storybooks, music tapes and art supplies, I prayed for God's help in teaching John about Jesus. But instead, John taught me about autism.

Evolution of Our Awareness of Mental Health
Dallas Morning News, February 15, 2010

The bible of mental illness, the *Diagnostic and Statistical Manual of Mental Disorders*, is being revised for a 2013 release. It will play a significant role in shaping policies in schools, workplaces and courts, and has huge implications for the insurance industry. For the first time, it may include individuals with autism spectrum disorders, which would have not been widely recognized years ago.[1] The Autism Society estimates that in 10 years, the annual cost of autism could be as high as $200 to $400 billion.[2]

Back then no one knew about "autism," or at least we didn't use the term. People considered John "retarded," and his parents never said much. All I knew was that this beautiful boy with the big brown eyes continuously rocked back and forth, sometimes banging his head on the wall. He never gave me eye contact, and he spent hours twisting pieces of string around his fingers. He didn't like to be touched and never spoke a word, yet God gave me a special love for John. He liked me, too, although I can't remember how I knew that. I just did.

Once, on John's birthday, I took a cupcake to his home. The house was neat, but in the corner of the dining room stood a tall cage-type enclosure made of wooden slats with a lock on the door. John's mom explained how they sometimes used it for John's own safety. Even as a young person, I understood that John's parents loved him, because kids like John were usually institutionalized. But the thought of that cage always haunted me.

Today, autism is out of the closet and making headlines. According to The Autism Society, 1 child in every 91 born in the U.S. will have some form of autism. The figure is 1 in every 150 in the general population.[3] This developmental disability affects a person's communication and social interaction. It is characterized by repetitive behaviors, restricted interests, resistance to change, and unusual responses to sensory experiences. Parents of children with autism grapple with early intervention programs. Doctors, teachers and therapists team up to support families coping with this ever-evolving diagnosis. Yet, autism is not a debilitating disorder. These children will likely one day be 60-year-olds with autism.

As Christians, we can't close our eyes to children with autism. We are called to have the same compassion Jesus had when He pulled the little children onto His lap and blessed them (see Matt. 19:13-15). Because we sometimes fail to see children with special needs through God's eyes, we can slip into the disciples' role of rebuking children. They just don't fit in— their needs and actions are different.

Making sense of autism is a daunting task. It's so multifaceted that it is considered a spectrum disorder. I thought of this when I read Frances Chan's book *Crazy Love,* in which he described God's innumerable designs in our universe. Chan points out that God didn't have to make hundreds of different kinds of bananas, but He did. He didn't have to put 3,000 different species of trees within one square mile in the Amazon jungle, but He did. God created a caterpillar's head with 228 separate muscles, and crafty spiders that can produce three different kinds of silk at a speed of 60 feet per hour. He even gave you and me goose bumps that cause the hair follicles on the back of our neck to trap body heat to keep us warmer when we're cold.[4]

Wow! God's designs are beyond our wildest imagination. The world's intricate beauty silences our finite thoughts . . . until we look deeper only to discover that all the "good" seems to exist alongside of the "evil" on our planet. For example, why are there so many disabilities, such as Asperger's Syndrome, Pervasive Developmental Disorders, and Rett Syndrome, which are all on the autism spectrum? Why do children experience uncontrollable behaviors, painful sensory issues, meltdowns and seizures? In other words, why *autism*?

Maybe you know of families whose lives are completely overwhelmed by the challenges of autism. You want to embrace them as brothers and sisters in Christ, but you simply don't know how to help. Or, you may be misinformed due to some common myths associated with a diagnosis of autism. Think about a time when you have felt misunderstood. Maybe a friend took your comment the wrong way or a coworker misquoted you in a meeting. Perhaps a Christian friend told you to consider it all joy when you face trials such as these because they produce perseverance (see Jas. 1:2-3). Now, imagine having a child with a disability that is so ambiguous that people actually point fingers at you—the parent!

Myths About Autism

Shrouded in mystery, autism makes parents of autistic children feel as if 1 Corinthians 13:12 was written just for them: "Now we see but a poor reflection as in a mirror. . . . Now I know in part; then I shall know fully." Someday, God's bigger plan will be revealed to all of us. For now, your friendship can comfort these families. And the first step is to dispel the myths about this disorder.

Myth 1: We Know the Causes and Cures for Autism

When children are diagnosed with any disorder, parents typically ask, "How did my child get this?" and "What will make him well?" For children with autism, these questions have yet to be answered. "We absolutely don't know the cause of autism," says Dr. Jeff McNair, Director of the Masters of Arts in Disability Studies at California Baptist University. "Autism is a spectrum disorder, involving a myriad of different disorders. There are therapies that can help, but no one therapy works across the board."[5]

A simple shopping trip used to result in a meltdown for nine-year-old Caleb Bundy. He would fall to the floor, screaming and slapping his honey-blond head. Caleb's senses became overwhelmed in busy, noisy stores. However, after four months of therapies such as social scripting and behavior modification, Caleb was able to enjoy shopping with his mom and brother. Like Caleb, Alessandro Barrero has autism, but he communicates his feelings with a picture exchange system, an alternative way of communicating without speech. And thanks to sensory integration therapy, Alessandro and his dad can enjoy playing in the park on sunny afternoons.

However, there is no one-size-fits-all approach. Even children with autism who are in the same family can have very different needs and interests. For example, consider the Anderson brothers, Joel (18) and Jared (21). Joel is nonverbal and has difficulty walking. He is hypersensitive and likes to listen to soft music. Jared is hyposensitive and wants his music loud. Joel's therapy includes a gluten-free diet, but diet changes didn't seem to help Jared. "You name it, we've tried it!" says their mother. Unfortunately, that statement is all too common among families coping with autism, and many times they feel as if they're grasping at straws.

Myth 2: All People with Autism Have Mental Retardation

Have you ever heard someone you care about called "stupid" or "retarded"? Has anyone ever made you feel that way?

Our culture often portrays children and adults with autism as stupid or mentally deficient, because they have difficulty receiving and processing information. Parents like Rosie Barrero, whose son Alessando has autism, take offense. "We're tired of hearing our children called 'retarded.' While friends and teachers don't use the word, it shows in their actions." Once, when Alessandro's abilities were questioned, the Barreros took a laptop to his school to demonstrate that he could read flash cards. Afterward, the school changed Alessandro's education program. "It's the saddest, most horrific feeling in your heart when someone doesn't believe in your child," says Mrs. Barrero. She wants people to know that children with autism are complete on the inside, and it's a tragedy to underestimate a child's potential. "I think that is what God meant in Proverbs 22:6, when He said train up a child in the way he should go," she says. "God's design for each of us is perfect."

An avid gardener knows that it's not about the hours spent weeding or watering—it's the thrill of watching a bud burst forth, or smelling a vine-ripened tomato. It's about an appreciation for potential beauty and flavor. But with autism it can be difficult to recognize the hidden treasures in the minds and hearts of these children.

In 1 Corinthians 1:26-27, Paul describes true wisdom: "Brothers, think of what you were when you were called. Not many of you were wise by human standards; not many were influential; not many were of noble birth. But God chose the foolish things of the world to shame the wise; God chose the weak things of the world to shame the strong."

Steve Bundy understands how someone can look at his son Caleb and think he is mentally retarded. "Sometimes a person will have a dual diagnosis; but to assume across the board that someone with autism also has mental retardation is just incorrect. It is a very different way of processing information and learning." Research has shown that a child or adult with autism can have a very high IQ, or even be a genius.

People with autism can learn. The question is, can we teach them? We can if we take extra time to break down tasks into bite-sized pieces, learn to use visuals and lots of repetition. We can if we stay flexible and refuse to give up.

Myth 3: All People with Autism Behave the Same

While there are similarities in learning styles and behavior patterns among individuals with autism, there is no way to determine how a person with autism will behave every time and in every situation. For example, Caleb must use a message board to ask for more grapes; but Jacob, who speaks clearly, often gets confused about what he wants to eat. When his mom presses him for an answer, Jacob would rather play than decide. Joel is on the other end of the autism spectrum and loves to talk about his art.

He began speech therapy to correct his "echolalia" (involuntary, repetitious sounds or words) at the age of two. Now, at age 15, Joel speaks to thousands of people through a foundation that demonstrates that people with autism can do many things.

Dr. Diane Cullinane, who is a Developmental Pediatrician specializing in children with autism, makes this observation: "These children have their own special interests and ways of responding to the world in terms of sound, movement—what they like to do and how they communicate. Their development is unique because their families are unique, as are the relationships within their families."[6] Clinical psychologist Ben Zequeira-Russell agrees, "I find that people on the autism spectrum have more of a diverse representation of capacities than those who are considered typical in their development."[7]

Myth 4: Autism Is Caused by Lack of Discipline and Poor Parenting
Most parents feel inadequate at one time or another. But for parents of children with autism, this feeling is reinforced by hurtful remarks from people who are simply ignorant about autism. As Christians, we must ask ourselves why it is so tempting to judge parents by their children's actions. Rosie Barrero confesses that she once vowed never to have an unruly child. That was long before she experienced her son's first meltdown at a Target store.

The myth that autism is the result of poor parenting originated with Leo Connor, who defined autism in the 1940s. Dr. Ben Zequeira-Russell disagrees with Connor, suggesting that many parents respond to their child's diagnosis by increasing their attention to parenting. Dr. McNair agrees: "Parenting is not a contributing factor to autism. Parents can be the most loving, affectionate, wonderful parents in the world, and their child will still develop autism."[8]

Sandi Anderson has grieved over rude comments about her sons, who both have autism. "Some whisper that it's the sins of the parents," says Mrs. Anderson. "One person asked why I would give blood, because of how my sons are—I've been stunned that people can be so mean." These comments hurt, but they can also cause parents to draw closer to God. They did for Mrs. Anderson: "Finally, the Lord calmed my heart, because He knows when I give the best that I can give each day. So, now when someone says something that stings, I know that tomorrow it will be a great story."

Autism requires that families ask for help, and there is no better place to go for understanding than the church. Right? It's where we practice being kind and compassionate to one another (see Eph. 4:32). We don't speak against our brothers or judge them (see Jas. 4:11). Alessandro sums up the care we must show families, when he says, "Be gentle!" So the next time you see a child throwing a temper tantrum in a public place, pray for that child and for his or her parent. Learn where there are parent support groups meeting in your community that you might recommend if the opportunity arises.

Now that we've dispelled the myths that can block our path to understanding autism, let's consider the truths that unite us in the Body of Christ. In Proverbs 24:3-4, we read, "By wisdom a house is built, and through understanding it is established; through knowledge its rooms are filled with rare and beautiful treasures." Let's consider how churches can become more welcoming when we treasure families affected by autism.

Treasured Truths About Autism

Christian friends can make a huge difference in the lives of children and adults with autism. Romans 12:5 says that "in Christ we who are many form one body, and each member belongs to all the others." For many of us this kind of "belonging" will require a major shift in our thinking, but the transformation can bring glory to God and a fresh maturity to the church. For example, if we think that individuals with autism can't understand spiritual truths, we'll miss the joy of teaching them about God. If we think they only want to be cared for, we won't experience the blessings that their love and service can bring into our own lives.

Sarah Stup, 24, is out to change the way we think about people with developmental disabilities. She declined typical employment options to pursue her passion for writing, and she has received several advocacy awards. Sarah is nonverbal and can't control her ritualistic behaviors. She has support that allows her to offer the world some amazing insights into autism. Here is an excerpt from her book *Are Your Eyes Listening?*

- I am inside.
- The words are there; the voice is not.
- It is lonely and sad not to talk.
- We who are silent have our value.
- Being autistic is a battle that stays.
- Your world hurts me.
- Sounds pay me visits after I leave them.
- I need autism to breathe.
- Autism is awful, but I am not awful.
- I act dumb, but am smart. Please be my friend.

- We can't be friends when you hate autism.
- Be an explorer who finds treasures beyond the strangeness.[9]

Sarah wants us to know that autism is part of a shield that she and others like her need. Without it, she wouldn't be who she is. You can read more of her work at www.SarahStup.com. Sarah is planting seeds of truth about this disorder, and they are blossoming.

Truth 1: Autism Separates Families from the Church

Have you ever felt painfully alone in a crowded room? If so, you've had a glimpse into the world of parents whose children have autism. These parents walk through our church doors every week, assuming their fellow worshipers don't understand their needs . . . and they're right! As a pastor of Christian Education for over 20 years, I've seen these families hurt emotionally and spiritually by our ignorance. We fail to notice that they can't always do what other families do. I have also watched autism's power drive a deep wedge between spouses, siblings, extended family and friends.

Autism is hard on parents who sometimes battle loneliness—even in their own homes. "What's really lonely is spending the day alone with Caleb," admits his mom, Melissa Bundy. "People don't understand how sad it is to not know what your child is thinking or to be unable to share your day with him." Parents, especially single parents who face these difficulties alone, can also feel guilty over not giving equal time to active siblings.

Dr. Scott Daniels, with whom I've served in two churches, has grown to appreciate the special needs ministry at his church.

"These families are limited in the places they can go within the community to find connection due to the challenges they face," says Dr. Daniels. "As our church truly becomes a genuine community, we're capable of bringing encouragement and healing. But I wonder what the prospects are for couples who don't have that unique community."

Surely these families are crying out as David once did in Psalm 142:4: "Look to my right and see; no one is concerned for me. I have no refuge; no one cares for my life." Julie Keith, director of In His Image at Dr. Daniels' church, is also concerned: "I know of churches that have not responded to these precious families as Christ would, and those families are no longer in church."

How can we get these families connected within our faith communities? Church consultant Barbara Newman recommends using glue. Yes, you read that correctly—G.L.U.E.! This acronym stands for Giving, Loving, Understanding and Encouraging. Newman worked with the CLC Network to create the G.L.U.E. Teams concept.[10] She holds seminars for churches, training them to do "ministry with" rather than "ministry to" those with disabilities. These techniques provide practical ideas on giving support to families where, when and how it's needed to allow them to fully participate in the life of the church.[11]

Truth 2: Autism Creates Fears that Christian Friends Can Ease
Remember dreaming about celebrating your sixteenth birthday, driving your first car and receiving your first real paycheck? Your parents may have worried about how you would handle new responsibilities, but they were also excited for you. The

worry and anxiety for parents of children with autism is magnified by the reality that their children may never even be capable of experiencing the most basic pursuits and privileges of life.

Brandi Urlaub is concerned for her son, Jacob. "My biggest fear is that it might be hard to find somebody who will really be there for Jacob," she says. "I worry about his safety and wellbeing if I'm unable to take care of him." Bill and Mika Buffington wonder if their son, Billy, will ever have a career and family. "I don't know who my son will be at age 25," says Mr. Buffington. "I'm dealing with today, but I don't know what tomorrow is going to bring."

None of us can know what the future holds for our children, and these fears can only be alleviated by truly embracing Christ's message of hope and peace. That's why God planned for us to grow and share in a community of fellow believers. "I try to remind myself that I have no control over the future," says Mrs. Buffington. "That's something that I continually pray about. I take all fearful thoughts captive and put them before God. He is the one who already has the blueprint." Mrs. Buffington's faith sustains her when she gets discouraged. She's learned to trust in God's sovereignty and lean on her church family.

Truth 3: People with Autism Can Know and Serve God

Some churches do an admirable job caring for children with autism but are unclear on what to teach. How much can they understand about faith in Jesus Christ? Since God created each of us with a unique purpose, we dare not underestimate the work of the Holy Spirit. "It's our spirit that comes to know God," says Julie Keith. "Our students with autism grasp God's love for them and how to share it with others. As I've watched them grow, I see that

His spirit is much more powerful than the human mind." Steve Bundy also sees this in his son: "Caleb needs a relationship with God as much as anyone else. It may look very different because he doesn't process information in the same way typical children do, but nevertheless, he needs spiritual instruction."

I've enjoyed spending time with Caleb, but the first time I came to his home, he kept his distance. He watched me when he thought I wasn't looking. He didn't respond to my questions or want to give me a hug when I left. But I wasn't discouraged. I knew that in time, if I let Caleb lead the way, I could show him God's love by being his friend. On a recent visit, we had a breakthrough. I entered his house with a gift box that I set on the floor. His curiosity drew him to the package, and soon we were both sitting on the floor touching the bright-colored paper. Then he lost interest and wandered into his room, waiting to see if I would follow. I did and took the chance to sing softly with the rhythm instruments from his toy box. At dinner, Caleb watched me and smiled when I included him in the conversation. He played with the wooden cars from the gift box. After his bath, Caleb snuggled next to me on the couch, putting my arm around his shoulder. As the family played a word game, he joined in with single-word answers, surprising all of us. Caleb's actions showed me that he felt loved and accepted, which was an answer to my prayers.

People with autism desire relationship. They need to see the evidence of Christ in our lives. Without that, how can they accept the gospel? "No one from the church has ever offered to help us," says Brandi Urlaub. "If I went to the church and asked for help, they might find someone available. But we haven't been going to church much because it's just too hard."

Families like these live in neighborhoods near your church. The Great Commission in Matthew 28:19-20 sends us out to make disciples of all people, teaching them to obey Christ's commands. "We misunderstand Christ's mandate when we allow the government to take the church's role," says Dr. Daniels. "We lose so much of who we are as the Body of Christ. We're people called to be salt and light in the world." While social services can help, they can never lead a child to Christ. However, when we go in Jesus' name, we can introduce a whole family to our Lord and Savior.

Truth 4: Autism Can Strengthen Faith Communities

We have seen the importance of embracing families affected by autism, but there is also a lot we can learn from them. "These families teach us how to love other people," says Dr. Jeff McNair, who teaches adults with disabilities at his church. "If someone comes to me with poor social skills, and I reject him, I've sinned—he didn't. So, if the Lord brings people into my life who are socially incompetent to teach me, then that is another benefit."[12] When we act with the mind of Christ, we have a tremendous opportunity to grow alongside these families. At whatever age a parent's child is diagnosed with autism, our response should be: "We don't care what your child's disability is; there's a place for you here." This goes beyond just providing childcare so families can worship, to helping them fully participate in our fellowship.

While leading a training seminar at University United Methodist Church in San Antonio, Texas, I visited their Helping Hands Ministry. This ministry is a group of young adults with disabilities who serve the needs of the church. Emily has hypersensitive autism and keeps to herself, but she likes to quietly straighten up and restock the sanctuary racks with envelopes, pens, hymnals and Bibles. Some days she fills children's worship tote bags with puzzles, worksheets and crayons. Another day she might prepare craft projects for preschoolers. But Emily doesn't like to serve at the Thursday senior adult luncheons, because she prefers to eat lunch by herself. Although Emily doesn't give eye contact or speak much, she knows she is needed at her church and everyone is glad she is there.

My friend Molly Kantz enjoys talking about the things her younger brother has taught her. In her book *My Brother Willson*, she describes him as an active nine-year-old who loves computer games, Bugs Bunny and karaoke! But he doesn't like being told no, or hair dryers, macaroni and cheese, or sounds he cannot control. Since Willson's kind of autism makes him hyposensitive, he likes touching everything, jumping on her and playing under the covers. She writes, "I am much tougher because of Willson. . . . I have amazed my friends with my patience. . . . I think God put autistic kids on earth to make us wish for heaven where everything will be perfect. . . . Even though I wouldn't choose for Willson to have autism, it has been a good influence on me and my family. I love my brother, even if he does have autism!"[13]

A special-needs ministry can touch the whole congregation. "As we see that God has well-intentioned plans for these children, it is transformational to us," says Dr. Daniels. "We have become a better people because we have this kind of ministry—living, laughing, and struggling together to become the Body of Christ. Without those challenges, we are just a group with like interests."[14]

Why Autism?

In the beginning of this chapter, I asked, "Why autism?" Let me suggest that God encourages our questions. Yet at the same time, He asks us to walk by faith. I can personally tell you that I feel God's presence when I spend time with families affected by autism, and they are changing me. But I'll turn to wiser people than me who have attempted to answer the question.

As a young child, Eric Hendrickson's autism diagnosis included extremely sensitive hearing; sounds were painful for him. However, what appeared to be a negative trait became an area of strength as Eric learned to cope with sounds. His keen ear led him to pursue language studies in college. In his high school valedictorian speech, Eric addressed the "why" question: "I was born with a serious handicap. . . . I have often been tempted to ask, 'Why can't I be more like everyone else?' This is when I must consciously remind myself of the truth that my life is not a mistake, God designed me JUST THE WAY I AM, and he has a purpose for me even in the things about me that are different. Perhaps especially in the things about me that are different. I have to make a conscious choice to believe what God's Word says is true about me, rather than believing what the world says about my value and importance."[15]

Joni Eareckson Tada says, "God made it clear that following Him would mean real hardship. Life is supposed to be difficult. More than that, it has been granted to us to suffer. Granted? Like a gift or a privilege? And what does 'for Him' mean? Problems are built into the Christian life for a privileged purpose. If we're to follow Jesus, we have to follow Him to Calvary. That's something God wants us to understand the moment we come to

Christ. God also wants us to realize it's a privilege to follow His Son this way. To follow Christ to the cross is to suffer for Him."[16]

Pastor Francis Chan concludes, "Whatever God's reasons for such diversity, creativity, and sophistication in the universe, on earth, and in our own bodies, the point of it all is His glory. God's art speaks of Himself, reflecting who He is and what He is like."[17]

Autism is one of the mysteries of faith. God chooses to use those who we perceive as "weak and less wise" to stretch us, mature us and teach us about His love.

Thank You, God, for parents who never give up on their children.
Open my mind and heart to see children with autism as You see them.
Use me to strengthen these families in my neighborhood and church.
Don't let me miss Your love shining through these precious children.
Amen.

STUDY QUESTIONS

1. Why is it so tempting to judge parents by their children's behaviors? What does this say about human nature?

2. How would you react if there were no cure for a disorder that you or your loved one was facing?

3. If you had a child with autism, how might your family's weekly activities change?

4. If you spent the day with a child with autism, what might be the most challenging thing for you?

5. How would you respond to someone who says that caring for children with autism is the job of the government, not the Church?

6. What qualities did you see in the parents in the chapter that you want to emulate in your own life?

7. Have your perceptions about individuals with autism changed after reading this chapter? In what ways?

8. What would practical support from your church look life for families affected by autism?

4

Self-Image in a Fickle Culture

By Joni Eareckson Tada

The easiest way to discover your self-image is to answer this question: What do you believe others think about you? Scripture tells us that our thoughts have power. Proverbs 23:7 says, "As [a man] thinks in his heart, so is he" (*NKJV*). So what is the tape that replays itself over and over in your head, and where did it come from? Jennifer Rothschild, a Christian author and speaker who lost her sight at 15, calls these inner thoughts "self-talk." She says we all have a silent dialogue going on with around 50,000 thoughts each day, and those thoughts can be constructive or poisonous, building us up or damaging us.

"Mirror, mirror on the wall . . . who's the fairest of them all?" Remember when Snow White gazed into the magic mirror and asked that infamous question? As a little girl, I sat in the movie theater, staring wide-eyed at the screen and thinking that Snow White was the most beautiful princess in the world. I remember coming home, wondering if there were such a mirror that might assure me that I was "okay," that I, too, could be lovely and fair above all. The idea was squelched the next day at elementary school. At recess I was teased incessantly about the shape of my nose. Someone would call from across the playground, "Look, it's a ski slope! Would you look at that? Her nose is shaped like

---

A Senate Chaplain's Self-Image
Christianity Today, June 2008

Richard Halverson struggled with an awful fear of inadequacy and an impulse to run away from responsibility due to his father's irresponsible behavior and failures.[1]

Amazon.com lists 1,496 books on the
subject of self-image.

---

an 'L.' " And if it wasn't my nose, it was "Get out of the way, here comes Horse-face!"

It's every child's nightmare. I know it was mine (and I bet it was yours, too). I'd look in the mirror and turn my head sideways as far as I could to critique the shape of my nose. And, yes, I loved horses, but returning to school the next day, I promised myself I wouldn't discuss horses with anyone, or draw them, or even check books out of the school library on horses. I didn't want to draw any negative attention. I wanted to be liked and accepted. I didn't realize it then, but I was doing what most young people do: *I was trying to understand my own identity on the basis of other's opinions and treatment of me.*

It's called self-image. Yet, it's often the opinions of others that provide the grid through which men and women construct their sense of self-awareness. A young person's self-image is especially influenced by the values other people place on his or her appearance, abilities, family background and environment.

This can be risky. Considering the values our society keeps pushing these days, it's little wonder so many people struggle with feelings of inferiority, insecurity and rejection of self. It's hard to maintain a healthy self-image in a fickle culture that idolizes a new tabloid star every six months . . . applauds the 50 pounds Dan Marino lost on Jenny Craig . . . will listen to your opinion only if you have a master's degree . . . or believes life hinges on whether or not Maybelline can luxuriously lengthen and thicken your lashes in just 30 days.

From the time we are very young, we are bombarded by messages from society that whisper, "Get thinner . . . be popular . . . get that 4.0 GPA . . . cover your gray . . . make that promotion . . . be the best ballet/karate/Little League/soccer mom in your neighborhood . . . and don't forget to whiten your teeth."

But what if . . .

- you can't lose those unwanted pounds?
- you can't keep up with Mrs. Jones and her ballet-twirling, soccer-ball-bouncing, karate-kicking kids?
- you were born illegitimately . . . or your father abused you?
- the Total Gym doesn't tighten your abs?
- you struggle with an addiction?
- you look in the mirror each morning and feel like a "hazardous waste dump"?
- you've been given a diagnosis of bipolar disorder?
- Head and Shoulders will never get rid of your scalp problem?
- your nose really *is* shaped like a ski jump?

Rejection and feelings of inferiority can easily topple your sense of wellbeing. Acne . . . a sordid family background . . . varicose veins . . . mental illness . . . crooked teeth. All of it is considered undesirable in a world that constantly pushes its values through its public institutions, including the media and magazines. No wonder so many adults struggle with self-image.

Kids Have Feelings, Too

Please don't think small children are exempt. Being "cool" is a prerequisite for acceptance by many elementary-age boys and girls. Most kids, at some point, have been teased by a sibling or a friend. It's usually not harmful when done in a playful, friendly way, and both kids find it funny. But when teasing becomes hurtful, unkind and constant, it crosses the line into bullying. Just look at the rise in incidents of bullying in school hallways. Almost 30 percent of youth in the United States—that's more than 5.7 million—are estimated to be involved in bullying as either a bully, a target of bullying or both. In a recent national survey of students in grades 6 through 10, 13 percent reported bullying others, 11 percent reported being the target of bullies, and another 6 percent said they bullied others and were bullied themselves.[2]

Sometimes the bullies are the adults. Whether it's an abusive parent, an overbearing coach or the cocky older brother, children are particularly vulnerable to accepting negative judgments from grown-up authority figures. Children don't know how to sift through others' opinions.

When my niece Earecka was in second grade, she loved to wear hats to school—whether it was her French beret, beaded Russian velvet cap or the embroidered hat her grandfather brought her from Norway, she proudly wore them all. That is, until her teacher teased her in front of her friends for being a "weird" kid. Earecka was wounded to the core. Although it is true that my niece was an unusual child, the fact that a respected authority figure labeled her as strange and peculiar hurt her deeply. That teacher sowed the seeds of self-doubt and self-consciousness in Earecka.

Scripture assures us that our words can have the power of life and death (see Prov. 18:21). God didn't entrust words to any other creature—only man! And the Bible is chock-full of warnings about controlling the tongue (see Jas. 3:5-12). Sharon Jaynes, in her book *The Power of a Woman's Words*, provides numerous examples of lives changed because life-giving words were spoken.[3] In one, she recounts the story of a young girl who had become the victim of Mildred, the school bully. When the mother learned of her daughter's pain and frustration, she decided to walk her to school and meet the troublemaker. What she found was a little girl, not dressed for the harsh winter, and looking in desperate need of love and attention. The mother knelt down, and instead of chastising Mildred, she bundled her up and asked if she would be willing to be her daughter's special friend? The mother then asked Mildred if she could count on her help. Mildred shook her head yes, and from that day on the two were friends and Mildred's entire countenance changed. In the simplest way, her value and worth had been confirmed!

What is "in" us that makes us readily reject others if they don't meet a certain criteria? What's at the core of our negative assessments about another's different habits, family background or their race or religion? Why do we feel "good" about other people's misfortune? Why do we feel better when we compare ourselves to those who seem less attractive or less intelligent than we are? It could be because we . . .

- Have a conscience that's been hardened by constant media messages.
- Have been raised under the influence of racial or religious prejudice.
- Feel more secure when others are made to feel insecure.
- Place inordinate attention on ourselves.
- Fail to appreciate the value God places on each person He's created.
- Have a fear of man rather than a fear of God.

Beauty and Brains . . . Is that All There Is?

With her thick dark hair, large eyes and porcelain skin, my friend Holly Strother is a striking beauty. A master's degree under her belt, a quick wit and a jovial personality make Holly the complete package, right? Yet Holly would be the first to tell you that she has yet to have a serious relationship. She has not found a young man who can see beyond her spina bifida, which makes her small in stature for her age. Holly walks with crutches and occasionally must use a wheelchair. But this doesn't stop her from working as a professional mental health care advocate.

In a society that airbrushes the images of even the most beautiful people, Holly finds herself longing for someone who can see beyond externals. For now, Holly spends her weekends with friends and family, striving to be content in knowing the lover of her soul, Jesus Christ.

I understand. Back in 1970, after I was released from the rehab center, I was one insecure 19-year-old in a wheelchair. My girlfriends, who wanted to help me quickly assimilate back into things, thought it would be fun to take me to the mall. They wheeled me into a boutique and helped me rummage through clothes racks to look for a blouse or two on sale. When they put me in front of a full-length mirror, I was horrified. It was the first time I'd ever seen myself from head to toe in my wheelchair. Up until that point, the image I had of myself only included what I could see of my lap, legs, and my feet positioned on the foot pedals. But in the floor-to-ceiling mirror, I was able to see that "Joni" now included a large, bulky wheelchair with a lot of paraphernalia on the back (the boutique's three-sided mirror provided a full view of what other people saw). I left the mall that day struggling to hold my head high. I even felt envious of the mannequins; clothes hung beautifully on them while blouses bunched around my waist and looked clumpy. Because I was sitting down, even the slacks I tried on fell high above my ankles.

I knew if I was going to emotionally survive in this new world of "sitting down," I would have to jerk my attention off of clothes and mirrors, and place it on something more exalted. The way I saw it, I had no choice but to gain a healthy self-image. It was either cultivate a positive self-identity, or fall back into defeat and depression.

The turning point came later when I attended a special seminar that was drawing national interest. It was Bill Gothard's Institutes in Basic Youth Conflicts: Research in Principles of Life.[4] Bill was a church youth director who had learned how to effectively help young people prize God and His values. He put those lessons into seminar format and, in the early 1970s, he spoke to huge crowds in convention centers across the nation. Bill Gothard revolutionized the thinking of a whole generation of young people like me, and the insights I gained helped me enormously. Even though I was still a novice in my wheelchair, I began to put into practice what I learned and was able to slowly develop a healthier self-image.

With Bill Gothard's permission, I'd like to pass on these key biblical principles on developing a healthy self-image in the hopes that the ideas will prove helpful as you counsel young people who are struggling with their identity. And who knows? These principles might even encourage you.

The Development of a Wrong Self-Image

A person's attitude toward himself has a profound influence on his attitude toward God, his family, his friends, his future and many other areas of his life. This may explain why so many people—especially young people—don't trust (or don't believe in) God, fight with their families, have so few real friends, and are anxious about their future. Simply put, they don't *like* themselves.

Our awareness of our own identity is greatly influenced by the values other people place on our appearance, abilities, parentage and environment. A negative self-image will be the result of accepting the values of people around us. When we compare ourselves to others, using society's yardstick, feelings of inferiority, insecurity and rejection begin to shape how we view ourselves.

I know a little boy named Ryan who has shiny blond hair, blue eyes and freckles. Ryan is one of the cutest kids I've ever met. You can imagine my surprise when I learned that Ryan used to sneak SOS scouring pads from under the kitchen sink and try to scrub off his freckles. He *hated* them. I'm not sure of the exact reason he despised those freckles, but it can probably be traced to comments from others—either kids teasing him at school or adults tweaking his freckled cheeks. Maybe his schoolmates conveyed that he was ugly; perhaps the adults made him feel silly. Whichever, Ryan did not like the way he looked.

Anyone can understand Ryan's struggle. Or, think about my friend Holly. If she were to use society's values, she would rate high from the neck up. But from the shoulders down, her body certainly doesn't meet the world's standards.

Evidences of a negative self-image:

- *An inability to trust God:* Our disapproval of our appearance profoundly affects our confidence in God. Very often a young person will be deeply troubled by his inability to really trust God. Try as he will, he just can't seem to muster the faith. He wants to rely on God, but can't. This inability to depend on God will very often be traced to something closer to home. Kids like Ryan will look into the mirror and think, *God is credited with creating everything, including me. He's also credited with being wise and loving. Well, if what I see in the mirror is an example of his love and wisdom, then I'm not interested!*[5] When we accept the values our culture places on our appearance and our abilities, we are quick to compare ourselves with others. This breeds feelings of insecurity and rejection. Little wonder it's almost *impossible* to accept the appearance or abilities God has given us. How can we trust the God who has made us "[His] workmanship," as it says in Ephesians 2:10, if we hate the finished product?

• *A resistance against authority*: When I was fresh out of the hospital and saw that many of my friends were beginning to marry, I found myself nursing hurt feelings. But I was only exhibiting what many of us often deal with; consciously or unconsciously, we feel that God "owes us." I assumed that since I had already been wronged once by the way God made me, I was not about to submit to further restrictions that might hinder even more of life's enjoyments. This lays the foundation for resenting all forms of authority. Looking back on those early days, I call that time my "rebellious period" in my wheelchair. I now cringe to think that I once enjoyed listening to '60s and '70s rock bands like The Rolling Stones and Jefferson Airplane.

• *A hindrance to genuine friendships*: Rejection of self results in a double hindrance to genuine friendships. It hinders our response to others and it hampers others' response to us. When we are oversensitive to the way other people react to our appearance or abilities, we become more focused on ourselves, and less focused on their real needs and interests. This concentration on the basic spiritual, emotional and physical needs of others is the foundation for building good friendships. At the same time, the negative feelings we have toward ourselves cannot help but be projected to potential friends. Occasionally, when my girlfriends spent time with me, I would engage in self-criticism in hopes that they would disagree and thus build up my self-image. But it backfired. A few of them sensed that I hadn't accepted myself as a quadriplegic and, soon, they tired of investing so much energy and effort into me. Thankfully, the others understood that I had a problem and were willing to stick with me and help me overcome my self-rejection.

• *A diverting of attention from true achievement*: People who struggle with their self-image are often motivated to compensate for their "deficiencies" by trying to achieve goals that will bring acceptance and approval from others. This desire for approval will often divert our attention from God's purposes and design for our life. True achievement involves the development of inward qualities that are consistent with God's character. "Man looks on the outward appearance, but the LORD looks at the heart" (1 Sam. 16:7). As true character is being developed, it will reflect outwardly, for "a merry heart makes a cheerful countenance" (Prov. 15:13, *NKJV*).

• *An overemphasis on materialism*: A very normal attempt to cover up our insecurities is to place an over-emphasis on clothes or other material possessions. The constantly changing fads and fashions in our society are vivid illustrations of this inner struggle. Remember my trip to the mall? I remember thinking, *Since I can't really control what happens from my waist down in this wheelchair, I'm going to control everything from my waist up.* I would spend days looking for just the right blouses and sweaters that didn't clump or look bulky on me, only to realize that these things do not really bring satisfaction. Jesus emphasized this problem while speaking to a group of His disciples. He identified their rejection of self by asking, "Who of you by worrying can add a single hour to his life?" (Matt. 6:27). And He observed their overemphasis on clothes when He asked, "And why do you worry about clothes?" (Matt. 6:28).

The Basics for a Good Self-Image

My friend Holly does a great job of holding her head high above the din of society's clambering media messages. She knows that a good self-image is grounded in a confidence in God's design and a new cooperation with Him. "I don't struggle with comparisons," Holly says. "Not with my friends, not with magazines or models on TV." Instead, Holly focuses on Jesus Christ (see Heb. 12:2). In Him, she finds the final guide for the qualities God wants to develop within her—qualities like gentleness and kindness, compassion and self-control. These are the things that make for a truly *beautiful* spirit. "If you live every day consumed by your disability, that's not freedom—that's bondage," she says. "But God gives you the confidence to be who you are!"

Holly has a clear understanding of God's design for her life. When she was working on her master's degree in social work at the University of Texas, she tried to find ways to reach out to others. For one of her classes, Holly and a classmate designed an online support group for young adults with spina bifida. It's just the beginning of what she dreams for herself in the future.

When we comprehend and accept the value God places on our appearance and abilities, we develop confidence in God's design, acceptance of our "limitations," and a happy anticipation as to what God will "do next."

How does Holly's situation speak to you? Would you like to share her confidence in God's design for your life? Would you like to walk into a room full of people and think, *Who here can I reach out to?* That's a much better response than worrying, *What will these people think of me?* Your self-image might be in need of a bit of improvement. If so, the following are just a few stepping-stones to achieve genuine acceptance of how God has created you, and what He desires to do in your life.

• *Begin a personal relationship with your Designer.* It's hard to appreciate what God is doing in your life until you begin embracing *His* values. It all begins with having a personal relationship with the God who created you, as well as His plans for you.

• *Thank God for what He is doing in your life thus far.* This is especially important when we realize that God is not yet finished making us. "We *are* [present, continuous action] God's workmanship" (Eph. 2:10, emphasis added). Psalm 138:8 says, "O, Lord . . . do not forsake the works of Your hands" (*NKJV*). The Lord has a long way to go to complete His design in your life, and He needs your cooperation to make it happen. Holly tells me that being alone on a Friday night is one of the crosses that she carries. But instead of getting bitter and depressed, she puts on her creative thinking cap. She loves to write; and so on Friday evenings, she blogs about disability issues on Holly's Heart.[6] It's become a great way to keep her focus on others, as well as partnering with God to more fully understand His design for her life.

• *Identify the root problem of a negative self-image*: How many young people do you know who are in need of a healthy self-image? Sure, many teenagers and young adults say they're okay, but stripped of their Facebook, iPhone, ability to text message, their cool clothes, the mall, and their friends, many feel emotionally naked and extremely vulnerable.

> *Surface problem*: Remember Ryan with his freckles? As he got older, his freckles never disappeared. This young man was continually criticizing himself and struggling with depression.

> *Surface cause:* As he grew, Ryan's freckles did too! When he became a teenager, he concluded that unreciprocated friendships were somehow connected to his facial appearance.

> *Root problem:* Ryan's rejection of himself reflected in unconscious bitterness toward God for giving him a face full of freckles.

> *Root cause:* Basically, Ryan was exhibiting a failure to comprehend God's values and purposes for the way He made him. It took him a while, but eventually Ryan learned to accept himself as he looked into the mirror of God's Word.

Obviously, the bottom line to gaining a confidence in God's design, as well as a thankful heart for His purposes in your life, is removing the root cause of the negativity. In Holly's life, the Bible became her guidebook for every healthy perspective and emotion. Her confidence in Christ rests on Psalm 139:14-16, where she learned that God designed *exactly* how she was to look even before she was born.

Next, Holly saw that her "prescription" of her appearance, as well as her disability, was logical if God had specific achievements He wanted her to accomplish (see Isa. 45:9; Rom. 9:20; 2 Cor. 12:9). The idea that God is not finished making her brought Holly a fresh sense of excitement and anticipation (see Eph. 2:10).

Holly's disability is like a frame around a piece of artwork. When a painting is completed, the primary focus should be on the actual artwork, not the frame. Likewise, Holly's disability "frames" the Christlike qualities that God is cultivating in her. When people spend time with Holly, they don't focus on the "frame" of her disability; they are drawn to the beautiful work of the Master Artist in her life. Holly's outward appearance will only continue to emphasize and enhance the godly qualities He will carry out to completion as she matures in her faith (see Prov. 15:13; 1 Pet. 3:3-4).

The Completed Picture

God's reputation is at stake in the masterpiece He is creating with each of our lives. When you think of it, the purpose of a beautiful painting is to be placed in a position of prominence so that many can admire and praise the ideas and abilities of the Artist. In the same way, I consider Holly one of the emerging new leaders in the disability ministry movement across the United States. At one of our Joni and Friends Family Retreats I saw Holly reaching out to other teenagers with disabilities. I could tell this was a young woman who truly *cared* about reflecting Christ to others. But it's an ongoing battle.

Television programs, advertisements and the covers of tabloid magazines are not about to soften their messages. They've been so effective that almost 10 million surgical and nonsurgical cosmetic procedures were performed in the United States in 2009.[7] The world is not about to lighten up. The "prince of this age" is constantly bombarding us with messages about beauty, brains, brawn, money and sex. No wonder the Bible warns, "For everything in the world—the cravings of sinful man, the lust of his eyes and the boasting of what he has and does—comes not from the Father but from the world. The world and its desires pass away, but the man who does the will of God lives forever" (1 John 2:16-17).

In the Christian's struggle to maintain a healthy self-image, we wrestle against . . .

- "The cravings of sinful man." Some translations of 1 John 2:16 say "the lust of the flesh" (*NASB*). Basically, God's Word is warning us not to be swallowed up by the cravings of the flesh or the competition to be more attractive by the world's standards.

- "The lust of his eyes." Our eyes are quick to examine the clothes and mannerisms, styles and habits of others. Such a focus only fuels our tendency to compare and compete. A healthier path is to fix our eyes on the One who is the source of beauty and wellbeing.

- "The boasting of what he has and does." The bottom line here is pride. So our struggle is to constantly look to God and His values and design for our lives. Otherwise, a root of bitterness will grip our hearts and we'll end up unable to respond to life according to the will of God.

First John 2:16-17 sums up the battle for all of us—especially Holly! She could have easily become embittered about living with spina bifida, but instead she is a testimony to embracing God's design, even in brokenness. Holly is a young woman who knows the source of true beauty—and it's not at the makeup counter. Holly's father says that her strength and faith throughout all of the surgeries and struggles she's endured have ended up making his daughter his hero. She continues to work hard not to compare herself to others.

How can we succeed in overcoming feelings of inferiority or bitterness toward God? Where do we start? With God's help, you can walk your friend, teenager or family member through the following steps:

- Acknowledge your bitterness toward God for the way He made you and ask Him to forgive you for not recognizing His workmanship in your life.

- Thank God for just the way He made you—Ryan ultimately had to even thank God for his face full of freckles!

- True commitment to God involves thanking Him for whatever the future may hold . . . or even thanking God for whatever responses others have toward us. It may give you the opportunity to share the love of Christ with that person who offends with his words or actions.

It's all about developing new thought patterns centered around the Lord and the values He places on our lives. It is rare to find someone who is basically satisfied with his appearance, background, abilities or life circumstances. We think we are either too short or too tall . . . too fat or too thin . . . too light-skinned or too dark-skinned . . . wishing we were single (if we are married) or married (if we are single). The future looks exciting when we are able to cultivate the discipline of building new thought patterns that reflect the value God places on our appearance and abilities. We come to appreciate the fact that He's not finished with us yet.

Fix Your Eyes on Jesus

Self-awareness, self-image and self-identity are all wrapped up in *Him*. And I mean that literally. Colossians 3:3-4 puts it this way: "For you died, and your life is now hidden with Christ in God. When Christ, who is your life, appears, then you also will appear with him in glory." Would you like to know who you *really* are? Who God has designed you to be? Well, as the Bible verse says, your life is "hidden with Christ." In other words, the deeper you delve into understanding who Christ is and what He values, the more you will understand yourself. Your identity is wrapped up in Him. Discover who He is . . . and it will put you on the path to self-discovery.

Little wonder the "prince of this age" competes so vigorously for your attention. No wonder he wants you to value the things the world values. His goal is to get your eyes off of Jesus Christ. But God tells us in Hebrews 12:2, "Let us fix our eyes on Jesus, the author and perfecter of our faith, who for the joy set before him endured the cross, scorning its shame, and sat down at the right hand of the throne of God."

Take time with the Savior and, as the old hymn goes, "the things of this world will grow strangely dim." Our world is filled with hurting, wounded people, and God has given you and me the marvelous privilege of being agents of change in their lives. He has called us to be extenders of His grace to both young and old alike. Let's agree together to make the gospel real in our world as we help the people around us look to Jesus Christ and the timeless values He places on our appearance and abilities, our background and environment.

God, forgive me for focusing on what others think about me.
My desire is to be the person You created me to be.
Only then can my self-image truly reflect You. I trust You to make
all things beautiful in Your time, including me.
Amen.

STUDY QUESTIONS

1. What aspects often contribute to a person's self-image?

2. Think of an area where you have been self-conscious. How did this make you feel?

3. How has a negative view of how you were designed affected your behavior and relationships?

4. What can you do to keep yourself from the destructive habit of making comparisons?

5. Where does your attention go as you study a piece of art?

6. Have you initially had trouble accepting a circumstance as God's design only to see later a bigger purpose than you could have imagined?

7. How can we hold to absolute truths regarding sin and share our convictions without fostering bullying or instigating hate crimes?

8. What changes about our confidence and self-image when we come to know Christ as Savior?

5

Searching for the Greater Good: The Stem Cell Debate

By Joni Eareckson Tada

Several years ago, General Motors launched a new campaign to generate sales with the slogan: "This Is Not Your Grandfather's Oldsmobile." Unfortunately, the ads alienated older car buyers and didn't attract enough younger ones, resulting in Oldsmobile's demise. Today, we face campaigns that make it clear: "This is Not Your Grandmother's Child." Some fertility doctors believe that parents will soon play a new role by designing their own children. The technology is called pre-implantation genetic diagnosis or PGD. It was created to screen for disease, then used for gender selection. In a few short years, some doctors believe it will allow parents to select physical traits such as eye and hair color—even freckles.

I love parking next to other people in wheelchairs and simply sharing *stuff*. The conversation almost always holds a surprise. Like the time I spent with Laura Dominguez. Laura, in her early twenties, sits straight and stately in her chair, the survivor of an automobile accident that left her paralyzed from the chest down. It happened shortly after her brother, Abel, picked her up after summer school. As they headed down the highway,

Why Lines Must Be Drawn?

TIME, August 23, 2004

When I was 22 . . . I suffered a spinal-cord injury. I have not walked in 32 years. I would be delighted to do so again. But not at any price. I think it is more important to bequeath to my son a world that retains a moral compass, a world that . . . recognizes that lines must be drawn and fences erected.[1]

Stem Cells to Cure Children of Chronic Liver Disease

The Times of India, March 21, 2010

NEW DELHI, INDIA—Children suffering from a chronic liver disease which causes irreparable damage to the organ may get a new lease on life as doctors have achieved initial success in their experiments with bone marrow stem cells.[2]

---

they could not have imagined what lay ahead. But when their car skidded on an oil spill, going 65 mph, and hit a concrete wall, so did Laura's bright future. The noise of screeching tires and crushing metal rang in her ears as she and Abel were rushed to the hospital.

At first doctors were hopeful, but then the prognosis became grim: Laura's paralysis would be permanent. Before the accident, she was an honor student with a zest for life. After the accident, her parents resisted the idea that nothing could be done to help their 16-year-old daughter. Laura felt the same way. She told me, "From the very beginning, I chose to fight back." She did just that. Every day in physical therapy Laura lifted weights to strengthen her upper body; she strained with all her might to try to learn to walk with leg braces. She did everything she could to gain back feeling and movement. But progress was slow.

Her dad was a fighter as well. Watching his daughter work so hard in rehabilitation with so few tangible results was frustrating. *There must be more I can do,* he thought. He wrung his hands and prayed, refusing to believe that God would want his beautiful little girl to remain confined to a wheelchair for the rest of her life. Laura's father began searching for whatever was needed to get his daughter back on her feet.

His search led him quickly into the world of stem cell research. He had heard that stem cells were the Holy Grail of miracle cures for all sorts of medical conditions. Could they hold the key for even hopelessly incurable conditions like spinal cord injury? Was this the answer for Laura? Mr. Dominguez began to dig deep into stem cell research studies. The more he read, however, the more he realized there would be no simple answer for his daughter's predicament. And he was about to learn why stem cell research is fraught with controversy.

Setting the Facts Straight

Everyone agrees that we need to find an effective treatment for Laura's type of paralysis, not to mention cures for diseases such as Alzheimer's, multiple sclerosis or cancer. And everyone agrees that stem cells hold the brightest promise for those cures. Stem cells are the body's "master cells," meaning they are blank-slate cells that are very pliable and have the amazing ability to morph into almost any other kind of body tissue.

Imagine the incredible possibilities! If your liver becomes diseased, doctors could conceivably "grow" new liver tissue out of stem cells to replace the part that no longer functions. If your heart muscle becomes irreparably damaged in a heart attack, simply replace the injured tissue with stem cells that will, with a little nurturing, transform into new heart cells. Everyone agrees that stem cells will play a key role in future medical therapies.

But people disagree on *which* kind of stem cell research to pursue. This is where the controversy comes in, because there are basically two kinds of stem cells retrieved from two very different sources.

- *Stem cells from adult tissues:* God placed within the human body its own supply of stem cells. The purpose of these stem cells is to repair and restore damaged tissue. The body manufactures these cells in places like bone marrow, nasal tissue, dental pulp, certain fatty areas, and blood. There are even stem cells in umbilical cord blood that seem to have special properties in morphing into other tissue. However, there are some limitations in the capacity of adult stem cells to take on all the characteristics of tissue in other parts of the body.

- *Stem cells in human embryos*: In the very earliest stage of development (the blastocyst stage), the human embryo is largely comprised of stem cells. Unlike adult stem cells, embryonic stem cells are specifically programmed to grow into certain body tissues. Some researchers are convinced that, despite significant problems in test results with lab rats, these stem cells are more flexible and are able to be nurtured into many more kinds of tissue. However—and this is the center of the controversy—researchers have to kill the human embryo in order to harvest its stem cells for experimentation.

As Laura and her parents educated themselves about treatments for spinal cord injury, they marched into a hotbed of controversy between medical science, ethics and theology. The scientific reality is: Researchers extract stem cells at their optimum moment for harvesting, but that kills the fragile human embryo. When Laura's parents learned this, they were deeply troubled. After all, they are genuinely religious people. "On one hand, we wanted to get Laura back on her feet," confided her dad. "We wanted to do whatever was possible to get her there. But if some of the procedures or research involves the destruction of human life, then that's going too far. We don't want to take human life in exchange for Laura to walk."

Cure or Kill?

Laura's mother and father found themselves anguishing over the question: Just how *sacred* is a human embryo? Medical researchers and many politicians would have us believe that a human embryo is just a mass of tissue. They try to strip it of its humanity by calling it nothing but a zygote or a blastocyst—they don't think of a human embryo as a *person*. And if it's not a person, it's not worth protecting. This is how many bioethicists and researchers are able to justify destroying human embryos for the stem cells. According to their way of thinking, it doesn't matter that it's a proven scientific fact that an embryo is a human being; that doesn't make it a person with moral and legal rights.

But what does the Bible say? Dr. Kathy McReynolds of the Christian Institute on Disability states, "What is clear from Scripture is that there is no such thing as a human nonperson. Every single human being from the moment of conception is a human person who has a fundamental right to live"[3] (see Gen. 5:1; 9:6; Ps. 139:13-16; Jas. 3:9). Because God made man in His image (see Gen. 1:26-27), human beings possess an innate and unique standing in all of creation—we are the only ones who possess an immortal soul.

This is what gives human beings their unique dignity. And because human beings are of *equal* dignity, we are not at each other's disposal (some say that if there were no "use" for human embryos in research, people would be more willing to grant it full moral and legal standing). When bioethicists and researchers try to separate *personhood* from a human being—no matter how small that human being is—they are undermining human dignity.

Just why is this so dangerous? If we violate the human embryo today, we become calloused about violating the fetus tomorrow, and then the infant, then the child with serious mental or physical defects, and then the adult in a coma. The human dignity of all weak and vulnerable people is terribly exposed in a society that thinks nothing of destroying human life for the sole purpose of medical exploitation and research experimentation. Like Laura Dominguez, I live every day with total and permanent paralysis. I am fully aware that people like Laura and I are exposed in a world where medical technology, not the Bible, sets the moral agenda.

Our secular society would disagree. They say that what does the most good for the most people should be the rule; that the needs of people with multiple sclerosis trump the rights of an embryo. But such an ethic breeds a society in which protection is based on power and one's ability to make a contribution. It's called "utilitarianism," and it's an ethic that while seeking to promote the greatest good is willing to sacrifice the weak and the vulnerable. The irony is that this ethic leaves little, if any, room for people like Laura Dominguez in her wheelchair.

On a strictly utilitarian basis, the resources devoted to caring for the severely injured could be "better expended" on those with prospects for a full recovery. Of course, we don't believe that. The fact that we don't operate that way is a testimony to what Christianity taught our culture about the sanctity of human life.[4]

Christians believe that there is something exceptional—even sacred—about the human embryo that sets it apart; hundreds of thousands showed this by signing the Manhattan Declaration. And whether or not we believe that a soul inhabits a human embryo, which most Christians believe it does, it is still not a goat, a chicken or a rat embryo. It is a *human* embryo. Each of us began our journey on this planet as one of those embryos, and life—no matter how infinitesimally small—is owed all the moral and legal protection that any human life enjoys.

Laura Dominguez's father and mother decided that stem cell research that used human embryos was not the answer for their daughter. But they were not about to give up. They pushed on, insisting, "We are not for destroying human life at all, but in the predicament that we are in, we'll give anything to get our daughter back on her feet. So what's it going to take? We don't want [researchers] to destroy a human life [in order to help Laura], but find another way to get around it!"

Another Way

Laura's parents turned their attention to medical therapies that used adult stem cells. What they found was surprising. They learned that stem cells from bone marrow have already been used successfully for many years to treat cancer and immune disease. A bone marrow transplant is, in fact, a stem cell transplant using the rich supply of natural stem cells found in the bone marrow. But that's not all. Adult stem cell research is on its way to helping the lame to walk and the blind to see in other ways—without destroying one life in the process. Consider a few of the successes:

- Bone marrow stem cells have successfully regenerated liver tissue.
- Adult stem cells are successfully treating kidney damage.
- Certain eye diseases are being reversed using adult stem cells.

- Adult stem cell therapies are in current trial or use for the treatment of certain cancers, autoimmune diseases, bone deformities, stroke and eye functions.

- At Duke University, children with cerebral palsy have been infused with their own umbilical cord blood stem cells ("banked" at the time of their birth) in an effort to heal and repair damaged brain tissue.[5]

The more Mr. Dominguez read about adult stem cell therapies, the more excited he became. In fact, Laura's search for a safe, ethical answer led her and her parents not only to a new therapy using her own stem cells, but to a new friend in Portugal, Dr. Carlos Lima. In groundbreaking procedures, Dr. Lima has helped restore muscle and bladder control in paralyzed people using their own stem cells from nasal tissue. After conferring with their doctors, Laura and her parents boarded a plane for Lisbon and the surgical hospital where Dr. Lima and his team worked.

After examining her, Dr. Lima decided that Laura would make a good candidate for his surgical procedure. In the operating theater, he removed stem cells from Laura's nasal passages, cultivated them, and then transplanted them back into her spinal cord at the point of her injury. Because they were Laura's own stem cells, they were genetically compatible with the neurons in her spinal cord, so there was no chance of tissue rejection.

After Laura came out of surgery, everyone held their breath. Before the stem cell injections, Laura could not feel her body, flex her wrists or stand using a walker. However, after the treatment, she had sensation in most of her body. This small but significant sign of progress spurred Laura to work harder in physical therapy. Eventually, she recovered good movement in her upper body, some bladder control, and some movement in her legs. She was even able to walk unassisted at the parallel bars. For her, it was a monumental and miraculous leap forward in her improvement.

The Rub of the Debate

With all the successes of adult stem cell therapies, why don't we hear more about it in the media? Good question. The biotechnological research engine is fueled by the need to find cutting-edge therapies that have the potential for profit (and which have the best chance of attracting scarce research dollars). So, all the high-octane effort gets focused on high-profile projects using the more enticing embryonic stem cells, while tough ethical questions take a backseat. The result is a flurry of reports about how embryos hold the key to future cures.

The Dominguez family was shocked to learn that no embryonic stem cells have been developed into medical therapies for people (as of this writing). It's too dangerous. Testing embryonic stem cells in animals has been fraught with problems. Yes, we see research videos of paralyzed mice that move their hind legs, but we're not told that those mice later develop tumors. God programmed stem cells in human embryos to grow, and they do just that . . . grow, grow, grow. The result? Massive tumors keep developing in laboratory animals that have been injected with stem cells from human embryos.

There's also the problem of tissue rejection. But scientists feel they have a way of overcoming that problem—cloning. The real push behind embryonic stem cell research is cloning. "What does *that* have to do with stem cell research?" First, I don't mean creating walking-talking clones like you'd see in science fiction movies; I mean something called "research cloning" (although scientists like to call it "therapeutic cloning"). How does cloning fit into our discussion? Remember, any medical therapy using stem cells has to be genetically compatible with the patient or else there's the problem of tissue rejection. That's a non-issue with adult stem cell therapies, but it *is* a problem for embryonic stem cell therapies. So how do researchers employ cloning to address the problem? Suppose you had a life-threatening liver disease. Doctors tell you they can completely replace the damaged part of your liver. Here's how:

- Scientists would scrape cells from your skin, extract your DNA, then insert your genetic information into a woman's egg (with its nucleus removed), and—*voila!*—create a clone of you!

- Your tiny embryonic clone would grow in a laboratory and, when it reaches a certain stage, scientists would harvest out its stem cells—cells that genetically match you.

- Scientists would then nurture and expand your cloned stem cells into tissue that could then be replanted into the damaged portion of your liver.[6]

- Because these cells would have the same extraordinarily flexible properties as any embryonic stem cell, you would have the best chance of replacing the damaged part of your liver with healthy tissue! Plus, there's no chance of tissue rejection. At this point, everyone would wait with bated breath and hope for a dream to come true.

But is it a dream, or a fantasy? Cloning humans sounds like something out of science fiction fantasy. However, if embryonic stem cell researchers have anything to say about it, it's the future. It's what will make embryonic stem cell therapies truly marketable to people looking for cures. If that's true, it is far, far in the future. Not only is the procedure of human cloning riddled with risks, but there are also huge obstacles that stand in the way of cloned cells leading to cures for *any* condition. Beyond the problem of tumors forming, as with any clone (such as cloning sheep or plants), there is the risk of short- and long-term genetic mutations. Not to mention the costs.

Scientists, researchers, the media and politicians nevertheless seem hell-bent on exploring the scintillating prospects of miracle cures through cloning. They talk of it as a kind of scientific destiny; that we simply have to "go there," no matter what the costs or risks. On the other hand, God states in Proverbs 14:12, "There is a way that seems right to a man, but in the end it leads to death." Not only death to embryos, but also death to a culture of life.

Yet there are valiant warriors out there on the front lines pushing back the tide. My paraplegic friend Jim Kelley testified before a U.S. Senate subcommittee when our Congress held hearings on whether or not taxpayer monies should be used to fund stem cell research that used human embryos. He stated, "The exaggerated 'promise' of cloning is not a path to cures in our lifetimes, but a dangerous diversion away from cures. It is in the interest of cures that I urge you to ban all forms of human cloning without exception."[7] Jim Kelley objects to embryonic stem cell research and cloning for practical and economic reasons. But the bottom line objection is still a moral and ethical one. The same ethic that tells us it's wrong to kill a human embryo tells us it's wrong to clone one.

Knowledge: A Double-Edged Sword

Who would have thought medical technology would bring us to this point? I wish the prophet Daniel could have lived to see this day. Then again, maybe he did. Perhaps he saw CNN in some prophetic vision and could only watch in wide-eyed wonder at all the increase of knowledge. Maybe his brain could only absorb so much until he heard God say, "But thou, O Daniel, shut up the words, and seal the book, even to the time of the end: many shall run to and fro, and knowledge shall be increased" (Dan. 12:4, *KJV*). Does the jet-blast speed of technological advancements mean we are close to the time of the end?

I can't say, but think of the time when human knowledge was just getting started. Genesis 2:9 says, "The LORD God made all kinds of trees grow out of the ground—trees that were pleasing to the eye and good for food. In the middle of the garden were the tree of life and the *tree of the knowledge of good and evil*" (emphasis added). We all know what happened next. A piece of fruit was plucked from the tree of the knowledge of good and evil. Man's innocence was stripped away and he was left bearing the responsibilities of knowledge—knowledge of what was good *and* evil.

Little wonder God wasted no time in taking action. In Genesis 3:22-24, "The LORD God said, 'The man has now become like one of us, knowing good and evil. He must not be allowed to reach out his hand and take also from the tree of life and eat, and live forever.' So the LORD God banished him from the Garden of Eden to work the ground from which he had been taken. After he drove the man out, he placed on the east side of the Garden of Eden cherubim and a flaming sword flashing back and forth to guard the way to the tree of life."

Some people think God was unkind in banishing Adam and Eve from the Garden. Some see the cherubim with the flaming sword as adding insult to injury. *Why would God make such a big deal about the tree of life?* Yet how merciful it was of God to keep sin-sick man from eating of the tree of life! Had Adam and Eve been able to make their way back into the Garden, mankind in his sad and sorry state would have lived forever.

It's clear from the first time the word "knowledge" is used in the Bible that it carries with it a sobering responsibility. It is a double-edged sword. Knowledge has a side that is good . . . and a side that is evil. It's been that way ever since the beginning. "The tree of the knowledge of good and evil" has a direct bearing on all that we've covered about stem cell research. Because for every medical advancement for good, there is always an accompanying potential for evil in terms of abuse—from splitting atoms to manipulating genes, from cloning to genetically designing the unborn child.

And add stem cell research to the ominous list. It has great potential for good—just look at how stem cells from Laura Dominguez's own body have benefited her! It also has great potential for abuse—just consider the thousands of human embryos that have been sacrificed on the altar of science thus far.

What of the future? Daniel the prophet echoes to us: "Even to the time of the end: many shall run to and fro, and knowledge shall be increased" (12:4, *KJV*). This is good . . . and not so good. As scientific knowledge continues to grow, we need Christians who will go before us and help lay the framework for prudent decision-making. When it comes to grappling with the essence of all that it means to be human, when it comes to killing embryos and cloning, let's remember we are touching a very peculiar fruit; not an apple hanging on a tree in a garden, but the apple of God's eye.

But Some May Say

Some people, however, are pragmatists to the core. They feel the research cat has already been let out of the stem cell bag, so why fight it? The embryonic stem cell industry is a multibillion-dollar business; the National Institutes of Health, in 2009, released dozens of stem cell lines (all from human embryos) for federally funded research. Why buck the trend? "Besides," pragmatists will say, "look at all the frozen embryos from in vitro fertilization clinics that are being discarded. Isn't it better to use them for research than throw them away? Those embryos are going to die anyhow."

That argument is a little like saying, "Death row prisoners are going to die anyway, so why don't we go ahead and put them under, and take their life-sustaining organs to benefit others?" Most people would find that suggestion morally abhorrent, despite the fact that there is a real shortage of organs for transplants. Similarly, it's wrong to kill tiny human beings even "if they're going to die anyway." We must not view human life as a commodity, but rather, promote ethical research that strengthens the moral fiber and caring character of society. We mustn't devalue the very human life medical science purports to help. It all boils down to how exceptional you believe the human embryo is—and Christians believe all life is sacred.

The pragmatist will still try to argue that we shouldn't use a religious ethic to critique science. The Christian worldview would have us direct our focus in these ways:

- Improve life—not attempt to create life
- Repair human life—not re-create life
- Work with nature—not power over nature
- Underscore Christ's healing—not focus on serving self

Laura Dominguez trusts that nothing can threaten God's plans for her. She reads her Bible daily and prays for people who feel they have no hope. Her desire is to keep others from suffering the depression she experienced, and so she dreams of opening a gym for people with spinal cord injuries. When she testified before the U.S. Senate subcommittee alongside Jim Kelly, Laura said that scientists have been given the knowledge and the tools to effectively use adult stem cell therapies, and that they should take full advantage of that gift. Laura and her family have the same determination today that they had when she was first injured, and they have vowed to never give up.

I've lived as a quadriplegic for more than four decades. It's been a long, long time since I have walked and been able to use my hands. It would be *wonderful* to be healed of my spinal cord injury. As an advocate, I interact with thousands of disabled people and their families; mothers and fathers of children with spina bifida, muscular dystrophy and juvenile arthritis. These families want the quickest and best path to take them from wheelchairs, walkers or white canes to a cure. This is why I support adult stem cell research, and the sky is the limit! Scientists are now working to modify the adult stem cell to give it special properties that will enable it to "act" like an embryonic stem cell, all within the safe boundaries of good ethics.

A scientific cure should be a hope-filled gift to the world, not the opening of a Pandora's box—and certainly not an affront to God's creative authority. God has not been ambushed by modern medical technology. He is the one who invented stem cells, especially the kind in our bodies whose purpose it is to repair and restore. Millions of people with serious medical conditions believe that adult stem cell research has the potential to be a true gift to the world. May God give us the wisdom and the opportunity to tell others the truth about where the *real* cures lie, and in so doing, safeguard the value of all God-given human life.

God, thank You for making our bodies so
wonderfully complex, with miraculous stem cells that
can heal injuries and diseases. Please give me the courage
to stand up for ethical research that will bless our children
and honor Your workmanship.
Amen.

STUDY QUESTIONS

1. How difficult would it be for you to handle a medical diagnosis of a disabling condition with an uncertain future?

2. If you were told that your only hope for recovery from a devastating disease was to have a stem cell transplant, what would be your initial reaction?

3. What are the two sources of stem cells? Which one has been most effective in bringing about cures?

4. How sacred are human embryos? Should scientists be allowed to decide when life begins?

5. Respond to this statement: "Good and evil are not matters of opinion but are based on truth."

6. If scientists could clone you and use your cloned cells to cure your disease, would you agree to the procedure? Why or why not?

7. As you consider competing opinions in modern society, how has Jesus Christ been your moral compass?

8. How would you address the subject of embryonic stem cell research with someone who is not a Christian?

6

The Truth Behind the
Pain of Abortion
By Sheila Harper

*After choir practice one evening, a good friend invites you to coffee.
You know she's under stress with three little ones and a husband who
travels a lot. You're surprised when she tells you she's pregnant and
her husband is pressuring her to have an abortion. As she tearfully
pours out her heart to you, which of these four actions do you do?
(1) Share Bible verses on the sanctity of life; (2) offer to go with her
to see your pastor; (3) tell her that abortion is a huge mistake that
she'll regret; or (4) Offer to go with her when she's determined to have
the abortion all alone? This is only one of innumerable scenarios
that surround this controversial topic, which reaches the very core of
God's design for the family. Surely He weeps with those who weep,
offering healing and forgiveness. Can we, His people, do less?*

—Joni Eareckson Tada

Imagine you're living the American dream. You have a devoted husband or a committed wife and a healthy, maturing
son. You're told there will be a new addition to the family and

Abortion Debate Gains Volume in Europe

USA Today, February 7, 2007

LONDON—The abortion debate in Europe, once largely settled in favor of liberal access, is reopening as anti-abortion groups gain strength and activists from the USA and other countries join the fight.[1]

you celebrate the upcoming arrival. The baby showers take place, bedazzling the nursery in pink. The heartbeat is normal, and the pregnancy is ideal. From aunts and uncles to grandparents and siblings, everyone adores the child already. The anticipated day arrives. Your tiny daughter takes her first breath, and everyone is ecstatic. But within hours, you're plunged into deep anguish. This precious child, appropriately named "Hope," is diagnosed with Zellweger syndrome, a disorder that stops the body's cells from ridding themselves of toxins. This syndrome is a devastating illness with absolutely no chance of survival. Now let me introduce you to David and Nancy Guthrie—they are that all-American couple whose world was turned upside down when what they thought would be one of the greatest days of their lives turned out to be the worst.

When the doctor sat across from the Guthries in the hospital room to convey the news, he didn't mince words. He stated the truth. No treatment. No cure. No survivors. Their precious baby girl would only live six months to a year at most. The Guthries, overflowing with sorrow, realized their dreams for

Hope would never come true. No tea parties, no senior prom, no walking their daughter down the aisle. They questioned how they would even exist for the coming months, knowing what they had to face. All they could do was accept the disheartening news and love their child one day at a time. They carried their cherished Hope home from the hospital and embarked on the task of caring for her as best they knew how. Less than six months later, they found themselves tackling the excruciating task of planning and attending her funeral.

Some might ask if the Guthries would have made a different choice had they discovered Hope's illness sooner. Would they have continued the pregnancy, knowing the pain they would endure? Society tells us abortion is an acceptable solution in these situations. But is it?

The Freedom of Truth

What is the truth behind the issue of abortion? Between the screaming politicians and the people carrying gory signs of aborted fetuses, there is truth. That truth is what we're going to find in this chapter. Tarry with me as we travel down a rough path amidst a difficult subject. We may be carrying lots of baggage at times, making our journey more treacherous, but stick with me. You'll be glad to discover the freedom of truth in the end.

The subject of abortion doesn't have to make you uncomfortable every time it's introduced in conversation. In fact, the mention of this word could put a smile on your face when you possess knowledge that helps others face this ugly issue. Don't skip this chapter, believing this subject is irrelevant to you. It's relevant to all of us. In fact, you likely have a close friend or family member who has faced this dilemma. "WHAT?!" How can I make this bold statement? Keep reading.

When abortion was legalized in 1973, very few people, if any, imagined it would develop into the industry it is today. Planned Parenthood is the largest abortion provider in America. In April 2008, their annual report revealed a total income of $1.02 billion. Taxpayers have provided more than $336 million worth of funding through government grants and contracts.[2] That means our tax dollars are being given to the largest abortion provider in the nation.

Since its legalization, tens of millions of abortions have taken place. Men, women and children have been affected. To be exact, when those numbers are divided among our population, we find one out of every four women has chosen abortion, which means one out of every four men has lost a child to abortion. If you know four people, odds are you know someone close to you who has an abortion in their past.

Many of us have believed the idea that abortion is an easy fix to the problem of an unplanned pregnancy, a pregnancy through rape or incest or a pregnancy with a handicapped child. There can be many reasons to make this choice, especially when presented in the form of compassionate, sound advice from a trusted doctor or friend. But there is an absolute truth. We can't shift our thinking for convenience' sake, or shun the truth. Sometimes facing the truth is hard, painful or even agonizing. But truth is still truth, and that's what we're seeking, because the issue of abortion is not going away. We can't pretend as if our hands are staying clean because we're ignoring abortion in our country. Regardless of what side you're on in this debate, let's dig deep and decide once and for all what we believe and how to apply that truth.

Where do you get your information? What has formed your opinion of the abortion issue? Have you believed only what society has instructed? These are questions we must consider as we seek the truth. Here are some familiar arguments we've all heard:

- It's a woman's right to choose.
- It's her body; she can do with it what she wants.
- I don't believe in abortion, but I'm not going to push my beliefs off on someone else.
- We should make abortion rare.
- I'm against abortion except in the cases of rape, incest or if something is wrong with the child.
- If the Supreme Court made abortion legal, then it must be all right.

These are all arguments that sound acceptable until you start applying moral principles and God's Word.

The last statement is what I believed regarding my own abortion, in 1985. I was 19 years old, but I knew something wasn't right about my decision. I rejected my own conscience. I sped past the warning signs. I didn't heed anyone's advice except those telling me what I wanted to hear. I let friends and society influence me to believe abortion was the easy way out of the problem. I assumed that if intelligent judges made it legal, then they must know something I didn't.

Now, although God has forgiven me and I walk free from my past condemnation, I still have unspeakable regret from that one choice made so long ago. My decision to abort was one I was not proud to share with my children, nor will I be pleased to tell my grandchildren someday. I'm ashamed because I didn't follow the truth outlined in God's Word—the truths that are written to protect us and provide safe boundaries.

When we search God's Word, we must recognize how He treasures life. Psalm 139:13-14 states, "You made all the delicate, inner parts of my body and knit me together in my mother's womb. Thank you for making me so wonderfully complex! Your workmanship is marvelous" (*NLT*). Those words do not reflect a haphazard creation. They're included in the Bible to let us know how closely God watches every intricate detail when He is creating one of His masterpieces. There is no creation of life made outside His ability. No life transpires accidentally.

So let's dissect these arguments we've learned from society and see what we discover. We hear that it's a woman's right to choose to do whatever she wants with her body. In most cases, I agree that she has this right. But society's laws would not allow that same woman to use her body to harm another individual. Why should a pregnant woman be allowed to harm the human living in her body? You may ask, "How do we know the baby is human?" What else could two humans make? Two humans cannot join and create something that is not human. If we're not certain this child is alive, then why not err on the side of life, as we would in every other circumstance. If someone were sick in the hospital, we wouldn't bury him or her because he or she "might" be dead.

Using the "woman's right to choose" argument has brought unspeakable pain into many lives. My friend Mark found himself in a terrible predicament when he could no longer deny that he had instigated and financed three abortions. He had believed that it was the woman's choice, and since he didn't want the baby, abortion was the best option. When he contacted me, Mark said he had "tried every program out there." He felt imprisoned by these three abortions and the pain he caused those ladies. I sent him our SaveOne Men's Study and prayed he would find the relief he needed.[3] He called two months later, and there was an amazing difference in his attitude. He had finally turned his shame over to God. Mark now lives free from past condemnation and has even started his own ministry, traveling and speaking about his experiences, and trying to keep others from making the same mistakes. There is hope and healing through God and His Word.

Some people may say they're against abortion but don't feel as if they can push their beliefs on someone else. What is it about the word "but" that relieves us of all moral responsibility? If this is your stance on the abortion issue, then I must ask: Why are you against abortion? Ponder that question. If you're against abortion, then you're probably against other immoral acts, such as spousal abuse, rape and the like. So use this same analogy with a different set of circumstances and insert the word "but."

I'm against husbands beating their wives, but I don't feel as if I can push my beliefs off on someone else.

I'm against rape, but I don't feel as if I can push my beliefs off on someone else.

Have I made my point? Why do we separate the issue of abortion from every other vile act?

There have been several politicians, from both sides of the aisle, proclaiming that we should make abortion rare. Again, I ask, why do we say this? If abortion isn't wrong, then why should we make it rare? Those same politicians wouldn't say we should make tonsillectomies rare. This question may be best answered by Dr. Alfred Bongioanni, professor of pediatrics and obstetrics at the University of Pennsylvania, as he testified to a U.S. Senate Committee regarding when life begins:

> I have learned from my earliest medical education that human life begins at the time of conception. . . . I submit that human life is present throughout this entire sequence from conception to adulthood and that any interruption at any point throughout this time constitutes a termination of human life. . . . I am no more prepared to say that these early stages [of development in the womb] represent an incomplete human being than I would be to say that the child prior to the dramatic effects of puberty . . . is not a human being. This is human life at every stage.[4]

Is this why we should make abortion rare? Because in the recesses of our minds we know it's a human life we're taking? We must recognize that this choice tarnishes the woman, the man and often their entire future.

Now, for the argument that convinced me to choose abortion: The Supreme Court legalized abortion, so it must be okay.

Let's look at another case that may shed light on this legalization. Back in 1847, a slave named Dred Scott sued for his freedom. It was 10 years later when the case made it to the Supreme Court, which declared this ruling: "Any person descended from Africans, whether slave or free, is not a citizen of the United States, according to the Declaration of Independence." They took a human being who was born in Virginia and made him a non-American simply because he was black, so the Declaration of Independence would not apply to him. The Supreme Court misrepresented what the Declaration of Independence said to fit the majority's desire—for black people to remain slaves.

On January 22, 1973, the Supreme Court made a similar ruling in the landmark case of *Roe v. Wade* that legalized abortion. They held that a woman is allowed to seek an abortion until the child is viable (able to survive outside the mother's womb). They defined viability to be 24 to 28 weeks.[5] Ironically, on the very same day, in the companion case of *Doe v. Bolton*, the Supreme Court ruled that an abortion could be sought to protect the health of the mother. The definition of "health" in this case was defined as "physical, emotional, psychological, familial, and the woman's age—relevant to the wellbeing of the patient. All these factors may relate to health."[6] So in other words, abortion was legalized on that day through all nine months of pregnancy. They made unborn children nonpersons simply because of their location and dependence on another human being. Therefore, the Declaration of Independence does not apply to children in the womb. The Supreme Court again misrepresented what the Declaration of Independence stated, to conform to the majority's desire for abortion to become legal in our country.

It's important for us to understand that the Supreme Court has been wrong before and they are wrong now. We look back on the years our country justified slavery with such disdain. We read about our country's history and wonder how our forefathers could have ever acted with such horrific behavior. Is that what our future holds? Will our children and grandchildren look back at us with disdain over this issue and wonder how we could have ever let this happen?

We Must Offer Something Better

You may believe that abortion is wrong but a girl or woman deserves a way out of a pregnancy if she is raped or a victim of incest. That sounds very compassionate. However, it's still a trap to ensnare us into thinking that does not line up with the truth of God's Word. So let's dissect this argument.

A young woman is the victim of a heinous crime: a brutal rape. It's the rapist who deserves to be punished, right? So why would we take this third party, the most innocent of all creation, and end his or her life? It certainly is not punishing the criminal. All this accomplishes is to turn the mother into an aggressor against her own child, thus heaping more baggage on top of the already horrible circumstances. Taking the child's life doesn't make the memory of the rape go away. In fact, if we would choose to trust God and His sovereignty, the child might become a bright spot the young woman needs in such a situation. God can take the most horrible circumstances and fashion the pieces into a most beautiful design. We *must* offer something much better to a rape victim than abortion. Life is valuable simply because every life is created by God. There are no exceptions in God's Word that make certain lives less valuable. Furthermore, Ezekiel 18:20 confirms the wicked will be punished for their wickedness and a child will not suffer the sins of his father.

I will admit that I have struggled with the cases involving incest. In Chattanooga, Tennessee, stands a landmark called The National Memorial for the Unborn.[7] It's an ex-abortion clinic, and the location where my abortion took place. Housed inside is a beautiful marble wall containing small plaques from various people who have bestowed honor to their aborted children. One of these plaques haunted me for many months. I still remember its words to this day: "To my ten children; incest was cruel to all of us." Reading those words always causes a lump in my throat. I honestly wondered how I would ever tell this woman that having these children was the right decision. I asked God repeatedly to help me with an answer. I just couldn't find it.

When I finally worked through my own emotions in this situation, God revealed the answer. When we allow an abortion to be performed on a victim of incest, we may be guaranteeing further abuse in her life. As long as abortion is readily available, the family secret remains safe and the girl's perpetrator can continue to abuse her. Ecclesiastes 8:11 says, "Sometimes the sentence for a crime isn't carried out quickly. So people make plans to commit even more crimes" (*NIRV*). And the *NIV Study Bible* explains that delayed punishment tends to induce more wrongdoing. If abortion were *not* readily available, there would be no way to cover up the crime. If this woman from the plaque had been allowed to birth the first child, the other nine abortions might not have happened. But, because he could repeatedly take her and dispose of the evidence, she was continually molested. First Samuel 2:6 says, "The LORD brings both death and life" (*NLT*). It is only up to our sovereign God to determine who lives and dies. Our lives are not about how we were created, but rather who we will become.

Submitting to God's Will

What about the other seemingly compassionate response to abortion in the case of a child being born with a disability? The Guthries are the most qualified to answer that question—and they have. Nancy said something that gripped me. She said they *submitted to God's will*. Read that sentence again. God's will. Wow. God's will has never included the promises, "You will never suffer, and you will never experience loss." What God's will *does* include is the fact that in spite of it all, He has a future for us, which includes prosperity, never harm (see Jer. 29:11). You may be thinking, *How in the world does this not contain harm? Where is prosperity in the loss of a child?* It comes down to the Guthries' response. They could have been angry toward God, or hospitalized their daughter and not enjoyed her short life. They could have blamed each other for the outcome and destroyed their marriage. But none of that happened. I'm sure there were flashes of anger and times of questioning God—they're only human. But in the end, they chose to submit to God's will and let Him be the sovereign God they had grown to love and serve.

Proverbs 16:9 tells us, "A man's heart plans his way, but the Lord directs his steps" (*NKJV*). I can assure you the Guthries' plans for their daughter, Hope, did not include disease and death. But they allowed the Lord to direct their steps. One of the questions Nancy asked was, "Do we want to insist to God that Hope's life has to be what we want it to be and what we've defined it to be? Or, has He created her uniquely, to fulfill a unique purpose? And rather than fight against that with our prayer, our desire was more to submit to it and to say, 'God, do something significant and show us how to make the most of every day we have with her.'"

How many times have we lived in a constant state of frustration because we're fighting God's will instead of surrendering? We may be placed in situations of suffering or we may be in a self-inflicted state of suffering. Either way, Jesus Christ is still the answer. His way, His will and His guidance are the only way to travel through the pain and come out on the other side better for it.

When I heard Nancy's words about submission to God's will, they instantly brought to mind Matthew 26:39, where we find Jesus in the garden of Gethsemane. Knowing the suffering He was about to endure, and intensely dreading the experience, He came to God: "O My Father, if it is possible, let this cup pass from Me; nevertheless, not as I will, but as You will" (*NKJV*). He didn't fight God's will; He submitted to it. He could have commanded all of heaven to His rescue. But He didn't. He could have pleaded, "Why me?" But He didn't. He could have proven Himself innocent. But He didn't. Because of His endurance in suffering, humankind can walk freely from sin today.

The Guthries' response was in many ways the same as Jesus'. We have much to learn from their reaction to Hope's diagnosis; but there's another part to their story that strikes at the heart of this question. We can't help but wonder if the Guthries would have made a different choice had they known of Hope's diagnosis before she was born.

In fact, we know what the Guthries would have chosen, because although they had taken precautions to prevent future pregnancies, they ended up facing the painful dilemma within two years of Hope's death. Nancy was pregnant with a boy, and prenatal testing determined that their son, Gabriel, did indeed have Zellweger syndrome.

When the geneticist asked the Guthries if they would like to discuss their options for the pregnancy, David assured the doctor there was nothing to discuss. "God has given us this child, not another one. We don't get to choose."

But how many times in our society have we been taught we can choose? If the pregnancy isn't planned, if this child was created through a vile act, if this child is not our definition of "normal," all reasons we've been taught are acceptable for abortion. We've had the authority of life and death handed to us, and many of us have chosen wrongly and suffered the consequences. That authority was never ours for the taking.

I'm sure that many people think the Guthrie family chose wrongly. Why bring a child into the world when it has no hope of survival? Why would someone put themselves through that kind of pain? Because the Guthries, although they anticipated the pain, also knew the joy their son Gabriel would bring. His name was so fitting. The three times Gabriel is mentioned in the Bible, he is bringing a message: "Do not fear!" The Guthries were convinced that God was going to deliver a very special message through their son, and indeed, since that time they have had the opportunity to proclaim the message through books and a national ministry.[8]

Steve Bundy, the managing director of The Christian Institute on Disability at Joni and Friends, summed it up perfectly: "If we allow suffering to define us, suffering will determine our attitude, our morals, even our ethics. But if we put suffering into the context of a sovereign God who loves, cares and is concerned for you and has allowed something to enter your life to make you a better person, to glorify Himself, to shape you into the image of Christ, then it brings purpose. It brings meaning to suffering, and we can find strength in Him to get us through the day." Nothing happens in our lives that isn't ordained by a sovereign God.

Although "sovereign" is the perfect word to describe God, it isn't the word commonly used. I believe that's because there are so few things in our life that warrant this title. Sovereign means supreme rank and authority. Nothing sneaks by Him. He is passionately interested in every facet of our lives. He has given us His sovereign Word to show us the path we must take. This path may have weeds grown over it because it's not well traveled. That's okay, the path is still there and it's yours to maintain. He always wants to take you on His journey to show you the best outcome in your circumstances.

An Earthquake Kind of Freedom

Another example of our sovereign God operating in an impossible circumstance is found in Acts 16. Paul and Silas were arrested unjustly, beaten to a bloody pulp, thrown into prison and their feet shackled. Where do we find victory in this story? Again, *it comes from their response.* In verse 25, Paul and Silas were singing hymns and praising God. What?! You mean after all they had been through they sang hymns and worshiped their Savior? Yes. They didn't question God; they submitted to His will. Verse 26 says, "Suddenly there was a great earthquake, so that the foundations of the prison were shaken; and immediately all the doors were opened and everyone's chains were loosed" (*NKJV*). The story goes on to say Paul and Silas led their jailer and his entire household to the Lord and baptized them as well. What a radical Christian life! How many times have we missed our earthquake-causing freedom because we chose the wrong path—the one society told us was right? Paul and Silas didn't resent their suffering; instead they found God in the middle of it.

Many men and women, like me, have chosen abortion and suffered greatly for it. But because of their willingness to deal with the pain and sin, Jesus healed and forgave them. Now those same individuals have a brighter perspective on life and are a light in the midst of the storm for many others struggling with the same heartache. Lives have been saved by the simple act of telling the truth about the pain abortion causes. This can only be done when a person is willing to see a purpose for their pain and find God in the middle of their circumstance.

When my friends Gary and Karen visited my office, they were broken. Their marriage was in shambles and their relationship with God could not have been worse. Karen discovered she was pregnant after undergoing an elective surgery. The doctor convinced her that their baby would be greatly disabled and the right choice was to abort. Gary remained quiet throughout the decision-making process, believing it was her right to choose. She quietly listened to the doctor, wishing the whole time her husband would rescue her. She chose abortion and that's when their lives fell apart.

As I worked through this process with them, I witnessed their painful submission to God's will. They turned all their hurt toward each other and themselves over to God, and He did what only He can do. He began to place the broken pieces of their lives back together into a beautiful mosaic. I will never forget the night they came in smiling, and in the middle of our session, Karen turned to Gary, took his hands and told him how sorry she was for blaming him. She forgave him and hoped he could forgive her. The relief on his face and the flood of emotion that filled the room was unforgettable. The pain had dissolved into the loving arms of our Savior. God is in the healing business, and regardless of the choices you've made, He can do the same in your life.

The Key to Victory

Like the Guthries, do you trust God to carry you through your circumstances? Even when you look around at your life and your current situation and cannot see how any good could come of it, will you rely on Him to help you through? Nancy Guthrie has another bit of wisdom: "Through experience you will know He is trustworthy. Sometimes we deem that trustworthiness is when the circumstances work out the way we want them to." Are you willing to take God by the hand and say, "You're will, not mine, Lord. I trust that You will take my situation and use it for Your glory and my ultimate good"? God can make a way where there is no way. He is going before you and chopping down all those weeds and obstacles that hinder. All you have to do is follow and believe He is working in you for His good pleasure (see Phil. 2:13).

What situation do you find yourself in today that needs God in the middle of it? Are you in an impossible situation similar to the one the Guthries found themselves in . . . *twice*? Or, maybe you're in a struggle of your own making. Whatever you're dealing with today, God still offers a way out of the pain. There is no sin too big that Jesus' struggle didn't resolve at the cross. His grace and forgiveness are for all of us, not just a few of us who "get it right." Make today the day you start believing the truth that never changes and always brings freedom.

The Guthries' pastor, Dr. Charles McGowan of Christ Presbyterian Church in Nashville, Tennessee, made the following observation: "We have questions. We have broken hearts, and all we have is the truth of the gospel, which tells us our Father would never hurt His children needlessly. Any pain carries with it a great fruit, and ultimately great blessing and growth."

There may be a situation in your life in which you may not have made a heroic choice like the Guthries, or like Paul and Silas; maybe your story is more like mine. You may be having a hard time forgiving yourself for some of the unwise decisions you've made in your lifetime. The choice of abortion isn't an easy fix that can be overcome effortlessly. You may have made the choice 3 months or 30 years ago. Nevertheless, it's okay to start the process of healing. God never intended for you to live your life in shame and suffering. Yes, we all make mistakes, but God's mercy is there and covers our sin. Today can be the day you turn your circumstances over to Him, because again, the answer is the same. Your response to pain and suffering is the key to victory. It's never too late to find God in the midst of your suffering. Take the pain and put purpose to it by turning it over to God. Your liberty is at stake. Your life is in the balance.

We praise You, heavenly Father, for the miracle of a tiny life. Forgive us when we fail to surrender to Your divine plans. Give us empathy for parents who suffer the pain of abortion. Empower us in battle to end abortion and to introduce families to You. Amen.

We pledge to work unceasingly for the equal protection of every innocent human being at every stage of development and in every condition. We will refuse to permit ourselves or our institutions to be implicated in the taking of human life and we will support in every possible way those who, in conscience, take the same stand.

—From the Manhattan Declaration

STUDY QUESTIONS

1. How do you feel when the subject of abortion is brought up in conversation?

2. What or who helped you develop your belief system regarding the issue of abortion?

3. How does Psalm 139:14 describe how each life is made?

4. What does "fearfully and wonderfully" mean to you?

5. What is one belief you have held to but now question because of what you learned in this chapter?

6. What is the "absolute truth" you can apply to that belief?

7. Tell why you do or why you don't believe the following quote from the Manhattan Declaration to be true: "A culture of death inevitably cheapens life in all its stages and conditions by promoting the belief that lives that are imperfect, immature or inconvenient are discardable."

8. How can John 10:10 be used as a "dividing line" in the Bible?

A Calloused Conscience: Eugenics and Genocide

By Joni Eareckson Tada

In 1988, I was a member of the National Council on Disability. I had been appointed to the 15-member council by President Reagan and then by President George H. W. Bush. It was the habit of our council to review scores of government reports relating to disability. In one particular meeting, we were reviewing a preliminary report submitted by the National Institutes of Health. Under the heading of "Disability Prevention," the NIH was considering the merits of abortion as a kind of disability prevention strategy. In other words, a disability like Down syndrome could be eradicated by encouraging more mothers to abort their "defective" fetuses.

Every year we look forward to Doug volunteering at our Joni and Friends' Family Retreats held for families of children with special needs. Doug is young and athletic, and a senior in college. The kids *love him* (and so do a few girl volunteers). When he first began volunteering, we assigned Doug to a little boy with Down syndrome. The two hit it off wonderfully. From that year forward, he always asked to be assigned to children with Down syndrome—he was drawn to their great attitudes and happy spirits.

**Parents of Down Syndrome Children
Divorce Less**
Vanderbilt Medical Center's Weekly Newspaper,
January 11, 2008

A Vanderbilt Kennedy Center study reports lower divorce rates in the Down syndrome group may be due in part to what the researchers call the "Down syndrome advantage," which refers to the personality and behavior of most children with the syndrome.[1]

Not long ago, I encountered Doug at one of our Family Retreats and he told me, "Joni, when I get married, I hope that my wife and I will have a child with Down syndrome." I was startled, but chalked it up to youthful idealism. I have come to see, however, that Doug meant what he said. He observed an unusual joy and guilelessness in children with Down syndrome. He could also tell they were a blessing to their parents.

I thought of Doug when, in 2007, the American College of Obstetricians and Gynecologists began recommending a broader prenatal testing for Down syndrome among younger pregnant women. Up until that year, they recommended that only older pregnant women be tested. After 2007, *all* mothers-to-be were routinely tested. And when given a Down syndrome diagnosis, *many* chose to abort their child.

Sadly, a woman's decision to abort can quickly morph into a social policy. It may be a worthy goal to do away with certain chromosomal defects; it's quite another thing to do away with *people* who have those defects. That's why all 15 members of the National Council on Disability were shocked by the National Institutes of Health's suggestion to consider abortion as a disability prevention strategy (it's interesting that we were a mix of Republicans and Democrats). We wasted no time in sending the report back to the NIH for revision. That was in 1988.

Decades later, it's quite a different story! The American College of Obstetricians and Gynecologists' guidelines are having a significant impact on the numbers of people born with Down syndrome. Recent U.S. studies have indicated that when Down syndrome is diagnosed prenatally, 84 percent to 91 percent of those babies will be killed by abortion.[2] That's aborting 9 out of 10 children! This trend is seriously altering our country's social policy. The watchdog group Physicians for Life states, "If current trends continue, it may eventually become 'unacceptable' for parents to continue a pregnancy knowing that their baby has Down syndrome."[3]

Perhaps you or someone you love has faced this dilemma. The outcome may have resulted in a quiet abortion. After all, matters like these are between a woman and her doctor. One would never dream that a personal decision like abortion would have any implications for human design. Oh, but it does!

This is what social engineering—or eugenics—is all about. It's a social policy that focuses on producing healthy, attractive, gifted children in order to have more productive and happier adults. The problem lies in the fact that healthy, attractive and gifted adults are, in fact, no more likely to be happy than disabled, unattractive or unintelligent people.

Take the example of my friend with Down syndrome, Robin Hiser. She is one of the happiest people I know, and I can't imagine how poor our world would be without people like her. In fact, it's well known that Down syndrome produces people who are generally happier than the rest of us! Although she has this genetic abnormality, Robin serves on the leadership team every summer at our Family Retreat in Pennsylvania. She has a passion for Jesus Christ and a deep desire to give the love of her Savior to other people like her. As Robin often says with a smile, "Worship of God is in my blood!"

Robin doesn't understand how to keep up with the Joneses or how to get over her head in debt. If Robin were married, she would not be clever enough to sneak behind her husband's back and look for an illicit affair (yes, men and women with Down syndrome do marry; and some of those marriages are honest-to-goodness models to neighbors and friends). Robin isn't cunning enough to know how to cheat, weave lies or stab a friend in the back. Best of all, she unreservedly shares her love for Christ with everyone she meets. If you ask her friends and family members, they'd tell you that Robin—like most people with Down syndrome—is the happiest person they know!

Survival of the Fittest

Back in the middle of the nineteenth century, Charles Darwin was beginning to write down his observations from his studies in nature. It was when he coined the phrase "the survival of the fittest." It was this idea that became the driving force behind his theory of evolution. Meanwhile, his cousin Francis Galton was toying with another idea. Galton theorized that you could make a better society if superior men and women were to marry each other and produce "more fit" children. It was Galton who coined the famous word "eugenics."

"Eugenics" literally means "good genes." If eugenics is a new term to you, it may sound like another miracle of modern science. After all, the idea of ridding the human race of defective genes sounds quite noble. Who wouldn't choose to have good genes or healthier DNA? Sadly, it can be more of a modern curse than a blessing. The idea of eugenics is as old as the Bible—ever since the beginning man has wanted to be perfect, to be like God. Humans have always tried to not only control but also conquer their environment to suit their ends—even if it means controlling genes!

I first learned about eugenics in high school. I was surprised, in fact, to learn it became one of the dominant movements in America in the first part of the century. I remember studying American posters exalting eugenics. One poster from the early 1920s showed a handsome, muscular farmer striding through a field scattering seed from his sack. The slogan on the poster read "Sow Only Good Seed." Our teacher also showed us that Alexander Graham Bell, the famous American inventor, was an early advocate of eugenics. In 1881, Bell determined that deafness was hereditary and noted that congenitally deaf parents were more likely to produce deaf children. In one of his lectures to the National Academy of Sciences, Bell suggested that deaf couples should not marry, thus limiting the numbers of deaf people in society.[4]

The eugenics movement was on a roll. Back in 1910, our government even opened the American Eugenics Record Office, which built card indexes based on the private information of millions of Americans, much of it obtained from hospitals without permission.[5] From the office's findings, more state laws were written to prohibit marriage and force sterilization of the mentally ill in order to prevent the "passing on" of mental illness to the next generation. These laws were upheld by the U.S. Supreme Court in 1927, and were not abolished until the mid-twentieth century. By that time, more than 60,000 Americans—many of them mountain people along the Appalachian Mountains—were forced to be sterilized.[6]

During this time, America was being closely watched by many leaders in Germany. But the Germans took eugenics much further. In 1939, the Nazi regime tried to exterminate the mentally ill and the disabled. They called it their "Euthanasia" program, but that was merely a euphemism. The program's chief aim was to "cleanse" out people considered genetically defective and a burden to society.[7] Once Nazi Germany adopted eugenics, they took it to its logical conclusion—the complete annihilation of *anyone* considered defective: Jews, Gypsies, the elderly, the mentally handicapped and people with disabilities.

With the close of World War II, many thought the eugenics movement had been dismantled as successfully as the concentration camps had been abolished. But did the movement really die?

Society's Calloused Conscience

It was 1982, and I'll never forget something that caught my eye in a newspaper. It was an article about a child with Down syndrome who was born with an obstruction in the food pipe. A simple, routine operation could have been performed by almost any surgeon within a 50-mile radius of the hospital, but the parents said no. They decided to allow their child to starve to death.

When word of the situation became public, a dozen families came forward and offered to adopt the baby, but the parents refused. Though it would have cost them no money, time or effort to allow someone else to raise their child, the parents, their doctors and the Supreme Court of Indiana said they had the right to starve the child to death. Seven days after his birth, Baby Doe died in a back room of the hospital. The U.S. Supreme Court never had time to hear the appeal.

I felt a little breathless, put the newspaper down and thought, *Then the life of every disabled person in the country is now at risk.* What was more troubling was the reaction by many pediatric surgeons. More than two-thirds stated that they would go along with the parents' wishes to deny life-saving surgery to a child with Down syndrome. Almost 75 percent said that if they had a child with Down syndrome, they would let the baby starve to death.[8]

Thankfully, it was a different story for Robin Hiser. Many years earlier, when Robin's parents learned they were about to bring a Down syndrome child into the world, they went to the Bible for guidance. Because Robin's condition had to do with a defective gene, Psalm 139:13 caught their eye: "For you created my inmost being; you knit me together in my mother's womb." They were able to lay the responsibility of Robin's chromosomal abnormality at the feet of God. It was God who was in control, and that was reason enough for them to welcome their daughter into the world.

Many people think a civilized society would never condone something as horrible as starving an infant to death (they call it "infanticide"). But in 1973, the Supreme Court of our land condoned the killing of an unborn child in a mother's womb, and the *Roe v. Wade* decision merely opened the door to devaluing all life. Once you abort an unborn child, society's conscience is more easily calloused toward an infant whose life is deemed not worth living.

I have traveled to countries in Africa, Asia and other parts of the world where infants born with spina bifida or Down syndrome are abandoned or discarded. Some infants are left to die solely because of a minor impairment, such as a cleft palate or club foot. In certain cultures, cerebral palsy is considered a curse from a witch doctor or from the animist spirits in the forest. I've talked with missionaries whose mission it is to rescue these infants and give them a home.

But disability is not the only reason infants are killed in many developing nations. Sometimes it's because of the sex of the child. The phenomenon of female infanticide has likely accounted for millions of gender-selective deaths throughout history. It remains a critical concern in the two most populous countries on earth: China and India. "Female infanticide," as it's called, reflects the low status given to women in most parts of the world where patriarchal societies dominate.[9] Many sociologists believe that the infanticide of girl infants in China and India will dramatically affect the delicate balance between the numbers of men and women in the future, making for a very unstable society.

Infanticide is not only practiced in developing nations; it's been made respectable in the West. The killing of "defective" infants has become legal in the Netherlands. At first, when Dutch doctors admitted publicly that they commit infanticide on babies with disabilities, the government's response was not to prosecute them for murder, but instead to urge that guidelines be created under which future baby killings could openly and legally take place. The Groningen Protocol—named after a pediatric hospital that admittedly permits doctors to end the lives of babies born with disabilities or terminal conditions—normalizes infanticide by bringing the practice out of the shadows and into the light of day. Under this thinking, it isn't the killing that is wrong, but the secrecy.[10]

Infanticide is only part of a much wider assault on God-given life. True, there was a time when the public would have been outraged over someone like Robin Hiser being starved to death, but the public no longer unites around the common moral premise that life is precious. Now, everyone does what is right in his or her own eyes (see Judg. 17:6). Social engineering, or eugenics, takes all sorts of shapes:

- Parents can now "design" their own babies, selecting the sex, hair and eye color and intellectual capacity of their unborn child.

- Elderly people are subtly pressured to forego life-saving treatment and honor their "duty to die."

- People with significant disabilities hear not-so-subtle cultural messages telling them one is "better off dead than disabled."

- Researchers continue to push to make cloned human embryos for experiments.

- Genetic engineering of human embryos may eventually alter human nature itself as changes in the germ-line are passed on.

Sadly, the strong moral fabric of our society is quickly unraveling right before our eyes. If only society would take the time to get to know—really *know*—a person like Robin, attitudes would drastically change. Once skeptics are able to look past foreboding statistics and unreasonable fears, they can't help but appreciate the value of someone like Robin and the way she enriches her family and community. She provides a living, breathing example of why it is a mistake to promote the social engineering of "happier, healthier adults" over the unborn and newborn with disabilities, or the elderly.

The Essence of Humanity

One quiet afternoon, my friend Stephanie Hubach was reading the Sunday newspaper when her eyes fell on an article, "The Toll of Alzheimer's Disease," by columnist Dr. Peter H. Gott. One paragraph read, "[Alzheimer's] eventually ends in a catastrophe: extreme confusion, loss of judgment, inability to recognize loved ones, belligerency, and the failure to be able to carry out everyday chores and activities of daily living. . . . In the truest sense of the word, the advanced Alzheimer's patient has lost all the qualities that make him or her human."[11]

Stephanie wondered how many readers would catch that last line. The columnist had reduced the essence of humanity down to a simple formula: "If you can stay focused, have good judgment, connect with your family, be cooperative, complete your chores and take care of yourself—then you are human. If you can't—then you are not. How many typical teenagers do you know who could meet those criteria?" Stephanie later observed.[12]

Gott's article reveals a growing cynicism in our society: People are being treated as *things,* not human beings with intrinsic value. We "have" no value because society no longer believes we are "created" or "made in the image of God." Instead, our humanity is shaped by subjective (not objective) values, such as one's comfort or another's convenience, or an ability to function or relate meaningfully to others. These values give shape to the *quality of life* ethic. Such an ethic extols the strong and minimizes the life value of the weak or fragile.

This raises the question: What *does* give human life value? God has placed something of Himself into human beings—something of essential significance that separates humans from the rest of creation. Theologians call this the *imago Dei* or "the image of God" in man. Human beings bear the imprint of their Creator. God made us in His image, weak and strong. We reflect Him in a way that other created beings do not. Stephanie Hubach, who is the mother of a boy with Down syndrome, reflected on the image of God in an article she wrote, "The Dignity of Every Human." Allow me to summarize her points:

- How human beings bear the image of God is *mysterious*—that's because God Himself is mysterious. The image of God, which we bear, is not easily understood because God is beyond our comprehension.

- We can acknowledge the image of God when we focus on the *goodness, loveliness and truth* that we see in each other, no matter what our beliefs.

- Because Christ is the image of God (see Heb. 1:3), *we also recognize His supreme worthiness in the life of all who re-*

flect Him, no matter how young, elderly or disabled the person may be.

- We also see God's image reflected in *relationships* (see Gen. 1:27). "Interdependent relationships between men and women operating in community . . . and particularly, within the Church, simply offer a broader perspective on God's image than when we image God in isolation."[13]

Whether God made us with genes that make life easy, or with genes that make life hard, is not the point. And neither is an elderly person's dementia or a young person's disability the point—our task is to treat *every* human being as someone worthy of the dignity God has granted each of us. As Robin poignantly says, "I just want to be treated like anyone else. I want people to know I'm a real person." That's exactly what Robin's friends and family do: She's included in all family activities; she is responsible for household chores; she goes to the mall with her friends; and she's one of the best leaders you'll ever encounter in a prayer group! When her father became ill not long ago, Robin even became his main caregiver. It's just like Jesus said: "When you did it to one of the least of these my brothers and sisters, you were doing it to me" (Matt. 25:40, *NLT*).

God's Image Reflected in Brokenness

Eugenics especially targets the weak and "defective." So for a moment, let's consider how the image of God is *especially* mirrored in the weak; that is, the medically fragile, the elderly or people with profound disabilities. Reflect on Genesis 32:25-32, where Jacob wrestled with the man of God and wrenched his hip out of socket. Jacob became one of the disabled, for the verse says, "he was limping because of his hip" (v. 31). When God met Jacob and left him wounded, it was a physical wound meant to remind him of his spiritual brokenness. He could no longer feign moral strength as he limped through life with his new physical disability. Dan Allender, in his book *Leading with a Limp,* says, "[Jacob's] limp is a reminder that when God renames us, He also makes each one of us a new person through a redemption that requires brokenness."[14]

God intentionally brings brokenness and weakness to those He loves. In fact, the biblical account shows that those God uses the most, He breaks for His sovereign purposes. And broken, weak people display the image of God most convincingly when they lean on Him for strength moment by moment. God's image is made most glorious when He is shown to be the one-and-only sustainer of those who are weak.

I've seen this in my own life as a quadriplegic. After living more than four decades in a wheelchair, I can honestly say that I would rather be in my chair *knowing* Him, than to be on my feet without Him. He is ecstasy beyond words, and it is worth anything to be God's friend—even quadriplegia. I've also seen how He's used my weakness in relationships. The people who help me with my daily needs have a glorious opportunity to follow in Jesus' footsteps and learn how to serve sacrificially (see Matt. 20:28). My disability provides the platform for not only my spiritual growth but also the growth of my friends and family, all to the glory of God. What could be more celebrated?

Weakness "fits" into God's grand scheme for His people—He allows the chromosomal defects for His purposes and He permits disabilities to occur as part of His glorious plan (see Gen. 50:20; Ps. 139:13; Rom. 8:28; Eph. 1:11). No wonder He stands in opposition to the sociologists, the biomedical engineers and the philosophers who fuel the eugenics movement. He says in Zechariah 2:8-9, "Whoever touches [the afflicted] touches the apply of [my] eye—I will surely raise my hand against them." When it comes to the so-called experts who push the idea of social engineering, Psalm 10:2 describes them well: "In his arrogance the wicked man hunts down the weak, who are caught in the schemes he devises."

Picture my friend Robin as you read Psalm 10:17-18: "You hear, O LORD, the desire of the afflicted; you encourage them, and you listen to their cry, defending the fatherless and the oppressed." Can you see how God is the champion of those whom society deems "unfit" or "unworthy" of life (see Deut. 10:18)? Psalm 9:11-12 tells us to "sing praises to the LORD. . . . For he who avenges blood remembers; he does not ignore the cry of the afflicted." And in Psalm 22:24 we see God's heart for the weak: "For he has not despised or disdained the suffering of the afflicted one; he has not hidden his face from him but has listened to his cry for help."

God is doing everything from His end to promote the sacredness—or *sanctity*—of all human life. He is bending over backward to defeat those who try to abort, euthanize, alter, clone or kill human beings. God is working to alleviate the burdens of the elderly, infirmed or disabled. He is laboring to lighten their load, protect their rights, safeguard their lives and preserve their dignity. God is working overtime to stop the hand of the wicked. But He requires His people to partner with Him: "Defend the cause of the weak and fatherless; maintain the rights of the poor and oppressed. Rescue the weak and needy; deliver them from the hand of the wicked" (Ps. 82:3-4).

Where Do Christians Stand?

Because we live in a fallen world with a distorted human nature, even Christians tend to extol the bright and beautiful, the gifted and the strong. Our natural reaction is to side with attractive leader types and ignore those we feel would drain our energies or require too much of us. First Corinthians 12:21 points out our tendency to exclude the weak or unlovely: "The eye cannot say to the hand, 'I don't need you!' And the head cannot say to the feet, 'I don't need you!'" Actually, we *do* need each other, especially when we consider how our relationships are a reflection of the image of God.

First Corinthians 12 goes on to say, "On the contrary, those parts of the body that seem to be weaker are indispensable, and the parts that we think are less honorable we treat with special honor. And the parts that are unpresentable are treated with special modesty, while our presentable parts need no special treatment" (vv. 22-24). Notice it states, "those parts . . . that *seem* to be weaker" and "the parts that we *think* are less honorable." From the world's point of view, people who are infirmed *are* weak and *have no* honor—that's the impetus behind the eugenics movement. But from God's point of view, these people are strong as they lean on Him (see 2 Cor. 12:11), and they have honor because they understand the source of their help (see Jas. 1:9).

Our nation desperately needs advocates for the weak. Remember earlier when I said that the Nazis did away with disabled people in institutions as part of their "euthanasia" program? What is striking is that Nazi medical teams entered those institutions and looked for disabled people who had no friends, no family members, no advocates or visitors. They selected only people who had no one to speak up for them.[15] Can you see now how important it is to be a voice for the weak . . . to speak up for those who are too small or too old to speak up for themselves . . . to voice a clear biblical worldview that extols the sacredness of all life . . . and to stand in opposition to those who would seek to diminish or even do away with anyone considered "too defective"?

If Christians don't speak up for individuals like Robin with Down syndrome who are being aborted, or for the infants with disabilities who are being starved to death, or for the disabled children who are being abandoned on river banks in developing nations, who will?! Who will speak for the elderly who are being rushed off to a premature demise? Who will stand firm and not allow so-called experts to dismantle the personhood of those who are too disabled or too elderly? Proverbs 31:8-9 tells us to "speak up for those who cannot speak for themselves, for the rights of all who are destitute. Speak up and judge fairly; defend the rights of the poor and needy."

Dark Forces at Work

Finally, our battle is not mainly against sociologists or biomedical engineers. It's not mainly against philosophers and politicians who are trying to subtly weave eugenics into a rational social policy. Ephesians 6:12 explains, "For we wrestle not against flesh and blood, but against principalities, against powers, against the rulers of the darkness of this world, against spiritual wickedness in high places" (*KJV*). I believe that Satan has always considered "infirmities" as his domain (see Job 2:4-7; Acts 10:38). It's a battlefield he thinks he rules. He uses everything from defective genes to dementia to try to usurp God's authority, destroy His creation and defame God's reputation (see Rev. 13:6).

However, there is nothing subtle about eugenics. We wrestle against a powerful adversary who delights in treating human beings as *things*. In John 8:44, Jesus calls the adversary a liar. Satan lies, trying to convince us that the elderly, or the disabled newborn or unborn have no *personhood* and, thus, no rights. In Revelation 12:10, Satan is called an accuser—he accuses, trying to convince mothers that it would be too burdensome to bring a disabled child into the world. In John 8:44, Satan is described as a murderer—he murders, pulling every feeding tube, pushing every injection of three grams of Phenobarbital, and cheering on every so-called death-with-dignity legislative bill across the nation.

Where Do We Go from Here?

We know who foments our "culture of death." *We* know who wants to touch the apple of God's eye, the weakest and most vulnerable. So we take a lesson from history, whether from Nazi Germany or America at the turn of the twentieth century. Then, we work to shake gospel salt and shine God's light into our communities, as we strengthen the fabric of our society.

Picture yourself at a community meeting or at a hair salon or in a discussion at a local health clinic when someone brings up the subject of "sex selection" of unborn infants as "the private right of any parent." Now you will be able to counter with an informed perspective. If your state assembly is considering a "physician-assisted suicide" bill, you can write your representative. Or, if a friend in your coffee klatch is thinking of terminating her pregnancy because of a Down syndrome diagnosis, you can compassionately plead for her to reconsider. We can strengthen our laws and relationships to safeguard the most important right—the right to life for the disabled unborn, newborn and elderly. If the rights of the weakest among us aren't protected, then *none* of us are safe.

The word "eugenics" may sound as though it belongs to the era of the gas ovens of Auschwitz, the pogroms of Stalin or the near annihilation of the Armenian people by the Turks. We may even think of more recent examples of ethnic cleansing in Cambodia or in Bosnia. But we have learned in our time together that there's another kind of eugenics that doesn't always grab the headlines or the attention of the evening news. Robin and millions like her stand in direct opposition to the modern eugenics movement. No one gives a more compelling defense for the sacredness of life than my friend with Down syndrome: Eugenics is *not* the answer for people like her *or* for the society in which she lives.

"But God chose the foolish things of the world to shame the wise; God chose the weak things of the world to shame the strong. He chose the lowly things of this world and the despised things—and the things that are not—to nullify the things that are, so that no one may boast before him" (1 Cor. 1:27-29).

God, help us see that all You created is good, because You
said it was good. Forgive us for thinking ourselves
better than others. Give us empathy for the millions who
innocently suffer and teach us to show mercy.
Amen.

Our concern is not confined to our own nation. Around the globe, we are witnessing cases of genocide and "ethnic cleansing," the failure to assist those who are suffering as innocent victims of war, the neglect and abuse of children, the exploitation of vulnerable laborers, the sexual trafficking of girls and young women, the abandonment of the aged, racial oppression and discrimination, the persecution of believers of all faiths, and the failure to take steps necessary to halt the spread of preventable diseases like AIDS. We see these travesties as flowing from the same loss of the sense of the dignity of the human person and the sanctity of human life that drives the abortion industry and the movements for assisted suicide, euthanasia, and human cloning for biomedical research. And so ours is, as it must be, a truly consistent ethic of love and life for all humans in all circumstances.

—From the Manhattan Declaration

STUDY QUESTIONS

1. How do you think you would have fared under Hitler's regime?

2. How do you believe our society views weakness compared to how God views weakness?

3. Did Robin Hiser's story dispel any preconceived notions you had about people with Down syndrome?

4. Robin calls her mother a hero. What do you think she meant by that?

5. What gives life value?

6. How would you summarize what the Manhattan Declaration says about life?

7. Now that your eyes have been opened to genocide and eugenics in both the past and present, what do you think about such manipulations now?

8

From Obscurity to Celebrity by Way of Tragedy: End-of-Life Issues

By Kathy McReynolds

When we first began plans to launch our Joni and Friends TV epi-sodes in 2007, I knew I wanted to tell Terri Schiavo's story. I was there with Terri's parents on the front lines during their struggle to save her life. I had to be there because so much was at stake. Where else would I be—not only as a person in a wheelchair, but as a Chris-tian? While judges deliberated, commentators interviewed so-called experts, and people marched with protest signs, it all came down to this question: Do we believe in the sanctity of ALL human life or do we believe in the sanctity of "some" human life? If the answer is "some" human life, who decides?

—Joni Eareckson Tada

Theresa Marie Schindler had an ordinary life growing up in the suburbs of Philadelphia. In fact, she might have lived out her life in obscurity were it not for her death. Born to Robert and Mary Schindler on December 3, 1963, those who knew

> ## Man "Trapped in Coma" for 23 Years Was Awake Whole Time
> FOX News, November 23, 2009
>
> Ron Houben, an engineering student, was misdiagnosed as being in a vegetative state after a car accident. Now, Houben (46) types on a computer that he screamed, but there was nothing to hear. And he literally never stopped dreaming of a better life the whole time.[1]

"Terri" describe her as a shy, slightly overweight little girl. She was the oldest of three children, and though she did not attend many high school dances or social events, Terri was very close to her family.

In 1981, when Terri was a senior in high school, her weight began to bother her, so she started a weight-loss program. By 1983, a much slimmer 19-year-old Terri was attending Bucks County Community College, where she met Michael Schiavo. To say it was love at first sight might be a cliché, but theirs was a whirlwind relationship. Michael proposed to Terri on the second date, and seven months later they married. It was 1984, and Terri worked for Prudential Insurance Company, and Michael was a manager at McDonalds.

In 1986, Terri's parents retired and moved to Florida. Not long after, Michael lost his job and the young couple asked if they could move in with the Schindlers for a time. Terri transferred her job to an office in Florida, and Michael found a good and stable job at a restaurant. Though they worked opposite schedules, and only saw each other on the weekends, the two seemed to have a close relationship. Terri and Michael moved into their own apartment in 1988 and started trying to have a baby. Terri had difficulty getting pregnant, so she sought the advice of an obstetrician. Terri held out hope, but after a while, it seemed God must have had other plans for them—a baby never came. Weighing in at about 110 pounds, Terri was still sticking with her diet, and in order to feel full, she drank several glasses of iced tea a day.

On Saturday, February 24, 1990, Terri attended church services with her parents; then they went to dinner and she went home. Terri told her parents she was not feeling well and planned to go to bed early. Michael was at work and did not typically get home until after midnight. Around six o'-clock the next morning, Michael was awakened by the sound of his wife collapsing to the ground. He called 911 after he found Terri on the floor not breathing. When the paramedics arrived, Terri had no heartbeat and no blood pressure. The medics spent 42 minutes trying to resuscitate her, restarting her heart several times. Though the paramedics were never able to normalize her blood pressure, they did finally revive Terri's heart.

When the police arrived at around 6:30 A.M., they found no evidence of a struggle in the home. Terri arrived at the hospital at 6:46 A.M. and subsequent blood work revealed she was hypoglycemic, but there were no signs of drug abuse. Terri never regained consciousness in the hospital, and her heart stopped beating several more times in the first few days she was there. Eventually, the physicians stabilized her and removed the ventilator. At that time, they also inserted a feeding tube.

Things Change

In April, two months after Terri's collapse, Michael had her transferred to a rehabilitation center. In November, Michael and the Schindlers took Terri to California and had a stimulator inserted into her brain. They brought her back to the rehabilitation center in Florida where physical therapists worked with her around the clock. Under their care, Terri made great progress. Michael was initially very supportive of all that the staff was doing for his wife. In July 1991, Michael transferred Terri to a skilled care facility where she continued to have the best therapy available for two more years.

In May 1992, Michael won a malpractice suit against the obstetrician who was treating Terri. The charge was negligence. After legal fees, Michael received $750,000 for Terri's care and $300,000 for loss of her companionship. It was at this time that Michael started to date other women. Tension started to build between Michael and the Schindlers. In 1993, three years after her collapse, neurologists told Michael that Terri would never make a "meaningful recovery." At that time, Michael agreed to the physician's request for a "Do Not Resuscitate" order for Terri. Terri's parents vehemently protested against the order, and Michael later cancelled it. Soon after, Michael requested that no more therapy be given to Terri.

The Schindlers became suspicious of Michael's motives and wondered if he might actually want Terri dead. They acknowledged that their daughter was severely disabled, but she was still very much alive. The Schindlers tried to remove Michael as guardian of Terri, but the courts continually blocked their requests. As the media became aware of her case, Terri's private life was catapulted to the world stage.

Life, Death and the Courts

Federal and state court involvement in medical treatment and end-of-life issues can be traced back most recently to Karen Ann Quinlan, in 1976, and Nancy Cruzan, in 1990. When 21-year-old Karen Quinlan overdosed on drugs and fell into a coma, she was unconscious for the most part but would occasionally have eye movement. Since she had some brain waves, she could not be declared brain dead. In 1976, the New Jersey Supreme Court set a precedent by allowing Karen's respirator to be removed.

In 1983, 24-year-old Nancy Cruzan lost control of her car on a country road in Missouri. She was thrown from her car on impact and landed face down in a ditch full of water. When paramedics arrived, they discovered that Nancy's heart was not beating. They immediately restarted her heart, but her brain had been deprived of oxygen for about 15 minutes, leaving her in a coma. For seven years Nancy remained in a coma, and over time her body deteriorated. Nancy's parents requested that the feeding tube be removed from their daughter; but the hospital repeatedly refused. The case was taken all the way to the U.S. Supreme Court.

At issue in Nancy's case was the constitutionality of Missouri law, which required clear and convincing evidence of a patient's desire to not be kept alive by medical interventions. Missouri's law claims a higher standard than "beyond a reasonable doubt" and the "preponderance of evidence," which is the standard in most states. The Supreme Court upheld Missouri's law, so Nancy's feeding tube was not removed. Nancy's parents eventually gathered enough evidence to satisfy Missouri's requirement, and soon thereafter, Nancy's tube was removed. Her case serves as an example of the kind of laws a state can pass in order to protect an incapacitated patient.

The courts affirm that all persons have the right to refuse life-sustaining treatment and that this right remains even if a person loses his or her decision-making capacity. The courts and relatives should respect and uphold the course of action the person would have chosen if competent. However, Terri Schiavo left no record of her wishes concerning medical treatment if she suddenly became incapacitated. Therefore, the courts in her case took care to explore the facts, including the appointment of three guardians ad litem. Over the course of several years, the District Court of Appeals of Florida rendered at least 10 decisions on various aspects of Terri's case. The parties sought review from the Florida Supreme Court four times, and the U.S. Supreme Court declined to intervene on four occasions.[2] Throughout the entire process, the courts never found Michael guilty of abuse or neglect.

On March 18, 2005, Terri's feeding tube was removed for a third time. The U.S. Congress and the president even intervened on Terri's behalf, but to no avail. The federal courts ruled that the removal of the feeding tube was "lawful and justified." Terri died of starvation and dehydration 13 days later.

More Questions Than Answers

Lawmakers and bioethicists have identified at least two primary competing interests in the Schiavo case. They are the "good" versus the "right" issue. The good is identified as the sanctity-of-life principle, and the right has to do with a competent person's right to refuse medical treatment, including food and water. The sanctity-of-life principle also involves a quality of life to a degree. Many ethicists and families recognize the right to take into consideration the kind of life a person in a persistent coma might have. Although these families are committed to the sanctity of life, they also want to know that their loved one is not suffering in any way.

Every year thousands of families face the overwhelming decision of signing a medical form that will end the life of a loved one. Terri's case became a media circus because even the general public took issue with many aspects of the Schiavo case, including: (1) confusion and lack of clarity in her diagnosis; (2) the withdrawal of nutrition and hydration; (3) who should have authority over life and death; and (4) the definition of a person.

1. Confusion and Lack of Medical Clarity

All parties involved gave conflicting reports concerning Terri's medical diagnosis and its meaning. Although the courts agreed with the testimony of capable neurologists that Terri was in a persistent vegetative state (PVS), other professionals questioned the diagnosis. Dr. Paul McHugh, University Distinguished Service Professor at Johns Hopkins University, points out that while an EEG and CAT scan showed significant abnormalities of Terri's brain, a functional assessment of her surviving cerebral tissue by use of MRI or PET was not used. The absence of such assessments was surprising to him.

McHugh recognizes that qualified neurologists examined Schiavo and that most of them concluded that her symptoms fit the description of PVS. He further states that the neurologists who coined the category PVS did so out of the best clinical motives. They wanted to distinguish it from the "brain dead" state, where no functional capacities remain. With brain death, a patient has no response to stimuli and the heart can continue to work only with the aid of machines. McHugh made this startling observation:

> By definition, then, PVS, is not death hidden by machinery. It is human life under altered neurological circumstances. And this distinction makes all the difference in how doctors and nurses think about it and treat its sufferers. The phrase "life under altered circumstances" encompasses every human sickness and disability. It also speaks to what is entailed in the professional art of medicine—the art, that is, of identifying and defending and, in the words of the Hippocratic Oath, "benefiting the sick." Given that doctors and nurses naturally align themselves with life, and are trained to care for whatever life brings, including "life under altered neurological circumstances," it is only to be expected that they would reject and shrink from actions aimed to kill.[3]

This insightful observation has implications for the remaining issues.

2. Withdrawal of Nutrition and Hydration

As stated above, there were many aspects of Terri's condition, which were unclear. However, it was clear that she was not terminal. She was not suffering. She sustained a severe cognitive injury that produced profound disabilities. This fact alone ought to give one pause to consider whether it was right to withhold nutrition and hydration from a person who was not close to death.

As soon as Schiavo's case went to court, the clinical concept of "life under altered circumstances" was completely undermined and so was the idea of how to serve such life. Both were eclipsed by the notion of "life unworthy of life." This phrase was a title of a book published in Germany in 1920, *Lifting the Constraint from the Annihilation of Life Unworthy of Life*. This is not to say that we have the sort of authoritarian government that Germany did at the time. The American way is much more subtle, relying on phrases like "upholding individual liberties, the rule of law, and respect for autonomy." Regardless of how it's worded, the outcome is the same. Michael Schiavo claimed to respect Terri's undocumented wish not to live dependently (life not worthy of life). Thus, the courts were willing to have her suffer pain, and by force of law to block her family from offering oral feedings of the kind even offered to terminal patients in hospice![4]

One of the fallouts of the Schiavo case is further discussion concerning the nature of artificial food and water. At least 12 legislatures in 12 different states are considering whether or not artificial nutrition and hydration (ANH) should still be considered a medical treatment or basic care.[5] The move toward "basic care" would be justified under disability laws. Disability rights groups such as Not Dead Yet argue that those in persistent vegetative states are not patients, but people with disabilities.

Catholic moral theology has had a tremendous influence on this issue. Traditional Catholic moralists did not deal with feeding tubes. They considered it a moral obligation to preserve one's life with food and fluids taken orally. They maintained that even food and fluids could be foregone if they failed to provide benefit. This view can be traced back to Catholic philosopher Francisco de Vitoria in the sixteenth century. De Vitoria's teachings on this subject were held consistently until 1980. The rationale has been that if it is true that orally ingested food and water can be refused, then it must also be true of ANH.

Since the 1980s, however, there has been a significant debate about whether ANH is a medical treatment or a form of care. If it is basic care, then it is always "ordinary" and thus morally required and can never be refused. Some argue that it is a form of care and therefore always ordinary and required. Others have insisted that it is a medical treatment and thus should be morally evaluated like every other medical treatment, especially given the fact that a feeding tube requires medical expertise in order to be inserted. As a treatment, burdens and benefits must be calculated in a patient-centered approach to decision-making. This view has historical precedent. Nevertheless, several Catholic Church documents indicate a shifting ground with regard to ANH. The current Catholic position is that ANH is a natural means of preserving life (form of care, not treatment) and therefore morally obligatory. This goes against the historical position.

Be that as it may, many Catholic scholars still argue that the criteria of the traditional moralists are valuable and should not be forgotten. Their position is as follows: (1) It is not how basic a particular means is to life or how commonly or easily available. Rather, what matters is whether the means offer a proportionate hope of benefit without imposing excessive burdens relative to the person's overall condition as judged by the patient; (2) Physical understanding of benefit is not the way traditional moralists understand it; the mere fact that a specific means is capable of sustaining life does not automatically mean it is beneficial or morally required. Traditional moralists include broader considerations—improvement, relief of pain, restoration of health.

3. Who Should Have Authority over Life and Death

Most Americans agree that medical decision-making should remain with the family. But, as the Schiavo case has shown, sometimes it is not that simple. Michael Schiavo had the authority to make medical decisions on behalf of his wife, and this ended in her death. One of the lessons learned from this case is the importance of making medical treatment wishes known. It is vitally important that everyone have an advance directive and appoint a healthcare proxy. This issue has enormous implications for the elderly and disabled, because there are concerns that those most vulnerable could be denied life-sustaining treatment. Disability rights organizations supported the Schindlers' quest to save their daughter. Terri's case also brings into focus the many problems related to quality-of-life judgments. Who should decide the quality of someone's life?

Prior to the 1960s, there is no reference to quality of life in medical literature, though it existed in other arenas. Why did we begin to see quality-of-life judgments in medical literature after the 1960s? The primary reason is advancing medical technology. Lives being saved now by medical technology could face chronic illness and disability. In fact, by 2050, estimates are that 120 million Americans will have some sort of disability. Thus, one of the purposes of quality-of-life judgments is to determine the limits of our moral obligations to preserve life. The second primary purpose is to determine the limits of medical intervention beyond what is beneficial for the patient. Still, there are legitimate questions concerning the meaning of quality of life. More clarification is needed concerning who decides and on the basis of what criteria.

One of the most important criteria to consider is the sanctity-of-life position. This position is found in both religious and secular texts. There are three main principles that flow from this position: (1) every life possesses inherent value; (2) every person is of equal moral value; (3) the quality-of-life ethic seems opposed to the sanctity-of-life principle. It is crucial to consider the goals of medicine as they are currently understood:

- To heal the sick
- To prevent illness
- To prevent disease complications
- To treat infections
- To improve functions
- To alleviate pain
- To prevent death
- To care for the dying

Withholding and withdrawing treatment interferes with these goals. The social commitment of the physician is to sustain life and relieve suffering. The American Medical Association makes clear that where the performance of one duty to patients conflicts with the other, the preferences of the patient should prevail. Physicians understand that the ultimate goal of medicine is to support, promote and advance the purposefulness of the patient's life. When medicine can no longer promote its ultimate goal of patient purposefulness at all, or when, by its interventions, medicine will place a patient in a condition that makes the pursuit too burdensome, then medicine has reached its limit on the basis of its own principal reason for existence and should not intervene.

But who should decide when this vital threshold has been reached? The patient, with caregivers, is the one who should decide on the basis of his/her values. When the patient cannot make the decision, then a legitimate surrogate familiar with the values of the patient should make the decision on the basis of what the patient would have wanted.

4. Definition of a Person

Many contemporary bioethicists justified the removal of Terri's feeding tube by claiming that she was no longer a "person"— that her biography was over. In fact, Michael had the following epitaph engraved on Terri's gravestone:

Schiavo

Theresa Marie

Beloved Wife

Born December 3, 1963
Departed This Earth
February 25, 1990
At Peace March 31, 2005

This idea that one could be a part of the human species and yet lose his or her status as a human person is a position widely accepted by many secular bioethicists. They would argue that medical advances now allow people to live who would not have lived in past generations. Whether at the beginning of life or end of life, one must now qualify to be considered a person. If a human being is not self-aware, able to make choices or able to value their own existence, then he or she is no longer considered a human person.

There is much at stake if this view of human beings prevails. First, from a legal perspective, if there is no personhood, cessation of care will not result in charges of murder or neglect. Second, from a social standpoint, families/physicians can become comfortable in accepting that the person is gone and further treatment is futile. Third, from an ethical viewpoint, if personhood ceases, no person exists to be harmed by nontreatment.

What Does the Bible Say?

From a biblical viewpoint, there is no such thing as a human nonperson. Scripture is clear that God's image is imprinted on every human being's soul, just as an image is impressed on a coin. It is a part of the human being's essence and can never be lost or diminished, and is not based on abilities. This view of the human person has the longest history in Christian theology.

Scripture's overall teachings indicate that human beings are not only *creatures* but also *persons* (see Ps. 139:13-16; Jer. 1:5). To be a person means to be able to exercise some independence, to be able to make choices, to set goals and attempt to accomplish them. In essence, to be a person is to possess freedom. Thus, the human being is a *created person*. This biblical understanding of the human being does reveal a bit of a paradox: How can a human being be both a creature and a person at the same time? To be a creature means to have absolute dependence upon God, while to be a person means to exercise relative independence. A creature cannot move or speak apart from God, but a person is responsible for his or her actions.

It is difficult to fully understand the mystery concerning how we can be both a creature and a person, but to deny either side of the paradox undermines the biblical teachings concerning the human being. Sometimes the Bible addresses human beings as creatures, as in passages like Jeremiah 18:6 and Romans 9:21; more often it speaks to the human being as a person: "Choose for yourselves this day whom you will serve" (Josh. 24:15); "We implore you on Christ's behalf: Be reconciled to God" (2 Cor. 5:20). Our biblical understanding of "human being" must keep both these truths clearly in focus.

Modern conceptions of human beings fail to take into consideration the creatureliness of the human being; instead they focus on personhood where freedom and choice are the defining features. Hence, from a modern standpoint, when one loses this freedom to choose, one loses something essential to his/her humanity. From a biblical perspective, this is a distorted and shortsighted view of human nature.

The Bible makes it clear that the created human person is made in God's image. After the Fall, however, this image became deeply marred. Human beings turned away from God and became His enemies by nature (see Col. 1:21). In the redemptive work of Christ, God graciously restores His image in human beings, making their will and desire one with His. Because we are creatures, God must restore us to His image through the work of sovereign grace. Because we are persons, we must become "imitators of God" (Eph. 5:1).

The Old Testament contains only three passages that specifically mention humanity as image bearers of God: Genesis 1:26-28, 5:1-3, 9:6. These verses lay a crucial foundation for understanding the rest of the teaching of Scripture concerning human nature. The first chapter of Genesis teaches the uniqueness of the creation of human beings. While each animal was created "according to its kind," only human beings are created in God's image and likeness. Herman Bavinck makes the following observation:

> The entire world is a revelation of God, a mirror of his virtues and perfections; every creature is in his own way and according to his own measure an embodiment of a divine thought. But among all creatures only man is the image of God, the highest revelation of God, and therefore head and crown of the entire creation.[6]

So, human beings, who are made in God's image and in His likeness, are His representation on earth, commanded to exercise responsible dominion over His creation. Genesis 5:1-3 and 9:6 make it clear that, even after the Fall, His image has been damaged, but is still intact. Only one passage in the New Testament clearly teaches that fallen human beings still carry the image of God, and that is found in James 3:9. James is not suggesting here that cursing is a sin only when it is directed toward believers; but he is saying that, whether a person is a believer or not, God is displeased when he or she is cursed, because that person is still His image bearer.

Thus, both the Old and New Testaments make it abundantly clear that human beings are made in God's image, and that image remains even after the Fall. Hence, to murder or to curse any human being is to sin against the Maker. In other words, it is an affront against God Himself.

Emmanuel

The New Testament also teaches that Jesus Christ is the perfect man—the ultimate picture of what God wants us to be like. It also portrays Him as the perfect image of God (see 2 Cor. 4:4; Col. 1:15). By reflecting on Christ as the perfect image of God, we can begin to see the relationship between the image of God and the Incarnation. Could the second person of the Trinity have taken on the nature of an animal? Not likely. John 1:14 teaches that the Word became human flesh. This presumes that because human beings are made in God's likeness, the second person of the Trinity could assume human nature.

If this is true, then the best way to learn about human nature is not to contrast human beings with animals, as is so often done within the context of medicine. Rather, we must learn what human nature is by looking to Jesus Christ. As we reflect on who He is, it becomes clear that human beings made in

God's image should not be defined or understood merely by their capacity to reason and make choices. When we examine what was foundational in the life of Christ, we discover that love is at the heart of understanding the nature of human beings. For no one ever loved as Christ loved.

Indeed, other virtues were evident in Christ's life, but love, as the New Testament teaches, binds them together in perfect unity (see Rom. 13:10; Gal. 5:14; Col. 3:14). In Ephesians 5:1-2, Paul says, "Be imitators of God, therefore, as dearly loved children and live a life of love, just as Christ loved us and gave himself up for us." The goal of the Christian life is to become more like Christ, who is the perfect image of God (see Rom. 8:29; 2 Cor. 3:18; Eph. 4:22-24; Col. 3:9-10).

The debate over end-of-life issues rages on. Many argued that removing Terri's feeding tube was the most loving act. Others sided with her parents, recoiling from the thought of letting a human being die of starvation and dehydration. Despite the claims of secular bioethicists that human personhood can be lost, there is no good evidence, scientific or otherwise, to suggest that this claim is true. It is an assumption they bring to the medical/scientific evidence that leads them to hold this view about personhood. Terri Schiavo was fully and completely a person until the day of her death. Now, according to her parents, she is a glorified person. She was not terminal, even though she might not have improved cognitively. There was much controversy concerning her precise medical diagnosis. We should have "erred on the side of life." The Schindlers, who loved their daughter, would have cared for her. Michael and the courts ought not to have been given the final say.[7]

Thank You, heavenly Father, for hearing the deepest cries of our hearts.
For it is with our spirits that we come to know You.
Grant understanding and strength to those who care for the helpless.
Remind us that what we do for the least of these, we do for You.
Amen.

STUDY QUESTIONS

1. Why do you think stories like Karen Quinlan's, Nancy Cruzan's, and Terri Schiavo's captured such national attention?

2. Following Terri's collapse, she was unresponsive for 42 minutes. Should the paramedics have continued to try to resuscitate her? Why or why not?

3. What were the two primary competing interests in the Schiavo case, according to lawmakers and bioethicists?

4. What is the proper role for the courts in our lives?

5. Is death a natural part of life, and what should be your attitude toward death?

6. Do you have an advance directive? Does the Bible give guidelines concerning whether or not to have an advance directive?

7. What are the goals of medicine, and why are those goals so important?

8. Should food and water be considered extraordinary or ordinary (basic) care? Why or why not?

9. Do you know anyone right now who might need someone to make medical decisions for him or her? How would you help that person?

10. How do we prepare to die?

I've Got Questions About the American Dream

By Steve Bundy

Just turn on the television, pick up the newspaper or flip through a magazine. The message is the same—buy, buy, buy! We live in an economic system of supply and demand, but for many it's never enough. The American Dream has become a nightmare of spending money we don't have to accumulate, use and store material possessions to improve the quality of our lives. So why aren't we happier? Nick Vujicic knows something about trying to fill life's empty places. Nick asked the question we all ask: "What is my purpose on this planet?" Nick's search led him to a different set of weights and balances and to the truth that only God can supply love, peace and a purpose.

—Joni Eareckson Tada

It felt like a scene out of *Outbreak*, a movie about a deadly disease sweeping the world. Our plane had just landed in Shanghai, China, and taxied to an isolated part of the runway. We sat in our seats for what seemed like an eternity until the outside hangar door opened for eight infectious disease agents. They wore full gear from head to toe with white outfits and helmets

25 million Americans (8.9 percent) are compulsive
shoppers/spenders.
Journal of Consumer Research, 2008

Men and women compulsively shop/
spend about equally.
Stanford University Landmark Study, 2006

Arguments over money are the number one reason
for relationship stress and break-ups.
Psychology Today[1]

that protected their airways from exposure. Upon entering the plane, they instructed all of the passengers to remain calm and explained that no one was to leave the plane.

The well-trained agents never said a word as they walked among the passengers, putting a device up to each person's forehead. Everyone, including me, was confused about what was happening. I noticed that the scanner they were using was actually an electronic thermometer that worked without actually touching the skin. It simply took a reading of the forehead, indicating the person's temperature.

Given recent world headlines and unprecedented panic in the U.S., I knew this treatment could only be the result of one thing—the Swine Flu. Fortunately, once every passenger had been checked, we were allowed to leave the plane and go to our respective destinations. Later, I learned that if one person had been running a fever, the entire crew and all passengers would have been quarantined for seven days.

The Silent Killer

As I reflected on my (almost) personal experience with a deadly virus, it occurred to me that a far more deadly "virus" has infected the human race. Its reach is truly global, and no one is immune to it. It is no respecter of race, ethnicity, age, gender or religion. Perhaps what makes it so lethal is that it's a silent killer. It gets so little attention that its victims are clueless about what has taken over their lives. This disease, which infected our first parents in the Garden of Eden, has infected all mankind. I'm talking about sin's effect on human nature.

Sin entered the world through Adam and Eve (see Gen. 3). Most of us have heard the story about how they hid in the bushes after they disobeyed God. Our first parents understood in an instant that they had lost their intimate relationship with God and with one another. God's perfection had been corrupted (see Rom. 5:12). Since then, sin has become a human pandemic! But do we truly understand its impact? Do we recognize how sin breeds selfishness, which infects us with greed? Maybe we need an electronic device like the thermometer to alert us when our everyday selfishness and greed start to morph into terminal materialism.

It's All Mine!

Ask the average Joe on the street about the human epidemic and he may throw out words such as "war," "disease," "murder" and "poverty." While these are terrible things, they're simply symptoms of the issue. Sin is the epidemic, and most people wouldn't mention it. That's because, like a virus, sin can be subtle and silent. It is not always blatant and obvious. That's the way Satan wants it.

In James 1:14-15, we read how temptation turns into sin: "But each one is tempted when, by his own evil desire, he is dragged away and enticed. Then, after desire has conceived, it gives birth to sin; and sin, when it is full-grown, gives birth to death." The chain is subtle.

Temptation mixed with desire ⟶ *turns into action* ⟶ *resulting in death.*

The difference from Adam and Eve and the rest of mankind is that we now have a sinful nature, whereby James indicates that our "own evil desire" entices us. The battle rages not just externally, but also internally.

This evil desire is "selfishness," and we all struggle with it. The root of sin is an internal desire to fulfill something for ourselves over and above what is good, healthy and beneficial. It is connected to the thought that "I" am going to experience pleasure by acting in this way, even at the expense of others. We are born with this disease. We're not taught it (fully), and it never completely goes away.

I have two sons of my own and have worked with children for years. One thing I know for sure is that we are born selfish. I've never had to take a two-year-old by the hand, walk him over to the corner and say, "Now, I know you really want to give this cookie away, but I want to teach you how to be selfish and not share with anyone." If you're a parent, I can hear you chuckling now. One of the first words out of our children's mouths is "Mine!"

The manifestation of selfishness is an obsession with material possessions. We see it in needless product consumption, overpaid sports stars or glamour shots in *Vogue* magazine. Americans have an overwhelming craving to "have it all." We live in a self-indulgent culture where most everything we could want or imagine is available. Combine such affluence with our love of *self* and you have what I call "the perfect storm" of raging materialism. For many the American Dream has become a dangerous game of spending more money than we make. Is it really necessary to accumulate stuff we don't need to improve our quality of life? If so, why aren't we happier? Why are many Americans taking anxiety and anti-depressant medications?

You may think that I'm being a bit harsh, and I understand. I, too, struggle with admitting my temptation to covet my neighbor's beachfront vacations, to obsess over my appearance or to draw attention to my own abilities and achievements. However, let's look at facts that have shaped behavior in our culture:

- By 2 years of age children recognize and ask for products by brand name.[2]

- By age 6, children can identify over 200 brand names, and accumulate an average of 70 new toys a year.[3]

- By age 8 to 13, children are watching an average of 40,000 commercials annually.[4]

- America spends $1 billion annually to dispose of food waste. If just 5 percent were collected it would feed over 4 million people for a day.[5]

- Nearly two-thirds of Americans are overweight, and we spend $40 billion annually in weight-loss products and services.[6]

- The average time spent shopping per week is 6 hours compared to the average amount of time of 40 minutes spent playing with children.[7]

- Americans can choose from 25,000 supermarket products, 200 kinds of cereals and over 11,000 different magazines.[8]

- Americans comprise 5 percent of the world's population but consume 30 percent of the world's resources.[9]

- Percentage of all humans who own a car is 8 percent; percentage of American households that own at least one car is 89 percent.[10]

- The world's wealthiest 20 percent consume 76.6 percent of all private consumption, while the world's poorest 20 percent consume only 1.5 percent of private consumption.[11]

One report indicates that the American attitude seems to be:

I can imagine it, therefore I want it.
I want it, therefore I should have it.
Because I should have it, I need it.

Because I need it, I deserve it.

Because I deserve it, I will do anything necessary to get it.

If this logic makes sense to you, I rest my case!

However, the problem is not with possessions themselves, but where we place our love and reliance. God has created all things for our enjoyment and blesses His children. We are to enjoy His creation. In 1 Timothy 6:9-10, Paul tells us the problem with materialism is not possessions, but love of possessions: "Those who desire to be rich fall into temptation . . . for the love of money is a root of all kinds of evil" (*NKJV*). Many people misquote this verse as saying "money is the root of all evil," but they're wrong. Paul emphasizes that it is the focus of the heart; it's about where you place your love.

What is the antithesis to selfishness? Paul provided the answer in 1 Timothy 6:6: "But godliness with contentment is great gain." That's right—godly living with contentment. Contentment (or lack of it) is the thermometer of our disease, indicating when the virus flares up and is running rampant. Selfishness creates greed and anxiety. Contentment produces generosity, satisfaction and peace.

Billionaire Howard Hughes had the world at his fingertips. He thought his money could buy it *all*—or could it? A successful film producer, industrialist, aviator and more, Hughes lived a life of luxurious pleasure. But swallowing the lie that more is better, his life ended in tragedy. In his last years he was a lonely, drug-addicted recluse. Instead of living a healthy, balanced life, the excesses that promised him pleasure brought only pain. At the time of his death, Hughes was unrecognizable. Drug use had depleted him physically to the point that the FBI had to resort to fingerprints to identify his body. His tall six-foot-two-inch frame barely weighed 90 pounds, and his hair, beard, fingernails and toenails were long and unkempt. Although possessions bring enjoyment, they cannot bring the contentment that satisfies the human soul.

But we don't have to have billions of dollars to fall into the trap of overindulgence. Following an afternoon of family errands, I felt a little sluggish, so I zipped into Starbucks and asked my wife, Melissa, if she wanted a coffee. My son Jaron immediately yelled out, "I'll take a tall hot chocolate." That's right! My seven-year-old knew the Starbuck's lingo. I suddenly realized that "hitting" Starbucks had become a regular tradition for our family. Glancing at Melissa, I said, "We're teaching our son that a lifestyle of $4 hot chocolates is normal." We immediately decided some changes were needed in how we teach our children the value of money and good stewardship.

Don't get me wrong. I'm not boycotting Starbucks or fun family time. We'll continue to enjoy these things, but in moderation. We weren't bad parents or intentionally seeking to be materialistic; but without even realizing it, we were slowly exchanging our values for those of others.

If we are not careful, worldly values creep in and change us into people we never intended to become. Our identity is defined by things instead of personal standards. Romans 12:2 says, "Do not conform . . . to the pattern of this world, but be transformed by the renewing of your mind." Selfishness and materialism are as old as recorded history. Let's look at three very different young men who struggled with these issues.

Misplaced Identity

Everybody loved Bill! He was kind, compassionate and generous. He volunteered at the local shelter and regularly attended religious services. Bill owned his own lucrative business, which he had built from the ground up. But over time, Bill became more and more consumed by his growing success. Relationships that he had enjoyed were being squeezed out for more pressing business. In truth, Bill loved the power and attention his wealth brought him. He became consumed with all he had and all he longed to achieve.

One day, Bill realized that life was passing quickly, and he felt empty and unfulfilled. He shared his feelings with a friend and asked him questions about where God fit in all of it. His friend read some Scripture with Bill, who could relate to much of what he heard. Bill thought maybe this God of the Bible could fill his emptiness. Then, they came across a verse that made Bill recoil in sadness, and left him wondering if he really wanted to become a Christian. The verse was 1 Timothy 6:10: "For the love of money is a root of all kinds of evil." Bill considered how much he loved spending money on his custom-made closet filled with designer suits and his classic car collection. He couldn't imagine his life without everything he had worked so hard for. He wasn't sure what it would mean to live a selfless life, but he decided that Christianity was probably not for him.

Bill's life parallels the story of the rich young ruler Jesus met one day. The ruler felt he had lived a good life, and he deserved the kingdom of God. When Jesus tested the young man's heart by asking him to give all that he had to the poor, the ruler's material possessions won out. His possessions were very different from Bill's, but the principle Jesus was trying to make applies. "No one can serve two masters. Either he will hate the one and love the other, or he will be devoted to the one and despise the other. You cannot serve both God and Money" (Matt. 6:24). Like Bill, the rich young ruler "went away sad" (Matt. 19:22).

Let's be honest. Most of us are thinking, *Yes, this all makes sense. I only want to serve one master. I want to be transformed and not conformed to the world, but why is it so hard?* One reason is that it takes us right back to Genesis 3. When sin entered man's heart, it destroyed that pure, unadulterated identity Adam had of being one with his Creator. The image of God in mankind was marred—not completely destroyed, but severely distorted. This loss of identity feeds our inner hunger—our desire to find wholeness in ourselves and even in material things. Like Bill and the rich young ruler, we let our identity mesh with our "must-haves."

Our lustful desires do not come from our heavenly Father, but from the tug of the world (see 1 John 2:16). The consequences that come from acting on these evil cravings are of our own making. Our fallen nature instinctively takes charge, unless we intentionally take action to be formed into the image of Christ.

If Only I Was Complete

Nick Vujicic is also a very successful young man. If I were to list his entire portfolio in this chapter, you would be extremely impressed. Nick is a successful businessman with a college education. He is an international speaker and author who has publicly addressed millions of people. He travels the world, meeting world leaders that most of us would jump at the chance to see.

His website gets millions of hits, and Nick achieved all of this before his twenty-fifth birthday. There is one other thing about Nick; he was born with no arms and no legs.

Growing up, Nick had questions. Lots of questions. "What is my purpose? What is my significance?" he asked, as he struggled with his identity. "I can see God's purpose for others, but not for myself. I can see significance in others, but not in myself." As Nick wrestled to understand why God allowed his disability, he developed an "if only" list for God. "If only God would heal me, then I could serve Him. If only I had my arms and legs, then God would be glorified."

Thanks to Christ's power to redeem and transform, Nick is not living a life of self-pity and complacency. Today, Nick speaks to millions who are trying to fill up their empty places. He explains how he found his identity in Christ when he stopped looking at what he didn't have, and started looking at what he did have. Nick's life is the antithesis to the millions of lives who search for "self" in material things. Nick knows that true identity is only found in a relationship with Christ.

In Colossians 2:9-10 it says, "For in Christ all the fullness of the Deity lives in bodily form, and you have been given fullness in Christ, who is the head over every power and authority." Now, you may want to read that again. Scripture tells us that Christ is the fullness of God—and that we are in Christ, and He is in us. If that becomes a reality to you and me, it can't help but transform us into people who are "in this world, but not of it."

In fact, Paul's theme for identity is that we are "in Christ" and no longer simply the selfish-natured people finding our identity in ourselves. He calls us "new creations." I challenge you to study Ephesians 1:1-14 and try to count on one hand the number of times Paul expresses the Christian's identity "in Christ . . . in Him . . . through Him." Depending on your translation, you will count at least 12 times in these 14 verses that he expresses our newfound identity in Christ. For Paul this was a reality. He called his ancestry, education, self-righteousness, abilities and possessions garbage compared to being found in Christ (see Phil. 3:1-11).

A Transforming Word

What about you? What's on your "if only" list? You may not face physical challenges like Nick or the parent of a child with a disability, but I would guess you have a list buried deep in your heart. Is it possible that your "if only" list is holding you back from finding your identity in Christ?

- *If only* I had that perfect job.
- *If only* my spouse was more social.
- *If only* I could lose weight.
- *If only* I had more money.
- *If only* I was smarter.
- *If only* we could buy the house we want.
- *If only* I had my friend's good looks.
- *If only* _____ .

It's not an easy question! It requires a great deal of self-inventory to compare your life with God's ideal plan for you. In Psalm 139:23-24 David asked, "Search me, O God, and know my heart; test me and know my anxious thoughts. See if there is any offensive way in me, and lead me in the way everlasting." Are there symptoms of a life that's gotten off track? Yes! Anger, pride, jealousy, lust and greed can all lead to broken relationships, sleepless nights and unwarranted spending sprees.

One of the fringe benefits of being a dad is that I get to watch all the children's movies (without actually confessing that I like them). It would be a little weird for a grown man to go see *The Incredibles* alone. One movie I really enjoyed was Disney's *Lion King*. It had all the characteristics of a "man" movie—war, romance and heroes.

If you saw the movie, you will remember the scene where Simba, the rightful heir to the throne of the tribe, went into hiding after his father Mufasa's death. After years of seclusion, his old friend Nala challenged Simba to return to the tribe to take his rightful place as king. But Simba wasn't interested in returning to face his fears. He had grown comfortable in his laid-back and self-absorbed lifestyle. In fact, Simba had adopted a new theme song, "Hakuna Matata," which means "no rules, no responsibilities, no worries for the rest of your days." He was so confused about who he was, Simba chose to remain in hiding.

Later, when Simba stopped to rest by a stream, he bent down to get a drink. In his reflection, he saw a vision of his father. Mufasa rebuked Simba, saying, "You have forgotten me." But Simba pled his case, saying that he had not forgotten his father. Mufasa's reply is almost biblical:

"You have forgotten who you are, and so you have forgotten me. You are more than what you have become . . . remember who you are, you are my son."

That's my favorite line in the movie, because Simba was transformed by the words of his father. The reality of Simba's identity was an epiphany that he couldn't ignore. He was the son of Mufasa, heir to the throne and leader of the tribe. Simba took heed of the haunting words of his father: "You are more than what you have become; you are my son!" Simba became a new lion with boldness, confidence and a sense of mission. He finally understood who he was, and what his life was about.

Blessed Assurance

So you may be getting a little concerned about my total recall of a Disney movie, but my point is: Have you heard your Father's voice? Do you know who you are and what your purpose is? Or is your identity defined by your neighbor's values, your investment portfolio or what's parked in your garage? And what happens if all the "stuff" is stripped away?

In Ephesians 1:4-5, Paul tells us that God chose us before the creation of the world, and He predestined us to be adopted as His sons through Jesus Christ. Let's look at four things your Father says about you: (1) You are an heir with His Son; (2) you are a worshiper; (3) you are a lover; and (4) you are a servant.

An Heir with Christ

Your true inheritance comes from God, because you are a child of God, and it has nothing to do with money! As a Christian, this is one truth that you can count on every day of your life. No matter your circumstances, mood or bank account, you have a Father who loves you. Yesterday, today and tomorrow, you belong to God. You were not saved to be a slave to fear, but you received the Spirit of sonship. Now you are an heir of God and a coheir with Christ. God is your "Abba Father" (see Rom. 8:15-17). The word "Abba" simply means "daddy." God holds His sons and daughters in the palm of His hand. Simply put, God owns it all, and as His child, you have access to His provision. Your spiritual and physical needs are met by Him.

Caleb, my 10-year-old son, was born with a rare chromosome deletion, which means he'll have lifelong disabilities. As a father, my desire is to provide for my son and care for his needs. He is my heir, and I am his daddy. This is intrinsic to me as a father, and I learned it from my own father. Before my dad passed away, he and I set up a trust fund that holds assets from his estate (and eventually mine) that will help provide for Caleb. It's not a large inheritance, but it expresses our love for him. As my son and my heir, whatever is mine is Caleb's. He does not need to live his life in fear and worry. And neither do we, according to Jesus' words to His followers: "So do not worry, saying, 'What shall we eat?' or 'What shall we drink?' or 'What shall we wear?' For the pagans run after all these things, and your heavenly Father knows that you need them. But seek first his kingdom and his righteousness, and all these things will be given to you as well" (Matt. 6:31-33).

When you know that you are an heir with Christ, you can live without fear of the future and without the need to grab and hoard possessions. Instead of living selfishly, you can be content and peaceful in the loving hands of your Father. And what does He require of you? Your responsibility is to look at how much you have been given and be prepared to give to others (see Luke 12:48). You also have a responsibility to manage your possessions in ways that reflect God's goodness.

A Worshiper of God

You were made to worship Him—not worldly possessions. Whatever you focus your heart and attention on is what (or who) you worship. As a Christian, you have the greatest privilege in the world: to worship your Creator. You bring glory to God through your words and actions, as well as your lifestyle.

One of my favorite stories in the Gospels is about the Pharisees who tried to trap Jesus in His own words by asking about the law regarding paying taxes to Caesar. If Jesus had said yes, it would have opened up a can of worms with the Jews who resented being under Roman rule. If He had said no, He would have been accused of leading a rebellion against the Roman Empire. In wisdom, Jesus asked to see a coin. Holding it up He asks, "Whose image and inscription is on the coin?" They replied that it was Caesar's. To which, Jesus responded, "Give to Caesar what is Caesar's and to God what is God's" (see Matt. 22:15-21). Just as the coin bore the image of Caesar, so mankind bears the image of God. Therefore, Jesus calls us to give to God what is God's. As His image bearer, you belong to God, and all of your worship is due Him as your God and Creator.

Worship is a lifestyle for Nick Vujicic. In many ways, Nick is a powerful picture of how one's life can point to God. Here he is with no arms and no legs, but he is living a useful, victorious life. His joy is so contradictory to what we might expect from a person in his circumstances, that even when he's center stage, it actually takes the spotlight off of him and magnifies the

Lord. It's what image bearers do: they glorify God. As the Lord spoke through the prophet Jeremiah: "Let not the wise man boast of his wisdom or the strong man boast of his strength or the rich man boast of his riches, but let him who boasts boast about this: that he understands and knows me, that I am the LORD, who exercises kindness, justice and righteousness on earth, for in these I delight" (Jer. 9:23-24).

Do you want to delight the Lord? Then do not boast in wisdom, strength or riches. When we worship God with our time, talents and treasure, He fills us with an overwhelming sense of contentment. We experience His pleasure in ways we've never dreamed of.

A Lover of God

You are to be a lover of God—not of self. A person is never as alive as when he or she is in loving relationships. Husband and wife, parent with child, friend to friend—life feels complete when relationships are healthy and loving. This is especially true when it comes to knowing the love of your Father. Being created in the image of God, it is only natural that you crave to give and receive love. John tells us that we love because God first loved us (see 1 John 4:19). His unconditional love draws you and teaches you how to love others.

Recently, I was with a group of Christian men discussing our understanding of God's unconditional love. One of the men expressed his struggle to believe that God could love him with all his faults and imperfections. I could relate to his struggles, and shared how my two sons have helped me gain a better understanding of unconditional love. As I mentioned earlier,

Caleb (10) was born with multiple disabilities, and he struggles with daily activities. My younger son, Jaron, hit all the development milestones early and has even raised the bar for other seven-year-olds (a little bragging from dad). Side-by-side there is no comparing their "performance." Jaron runs circles around his older brother. But, if you asked me who I love most, I would respond that I love them both equally. If my love were based on performance, I would love Jaron more than Caleb. But my love for my sons is not based on their performance . . . my love is as unconditional for them as humanly possible. I think this is a glimpse of God's unconditional love for us.

When you know and experience God's love, you can love others with passion. You can take the focus off of yourself and place it on others, defeating selfishness. God's love in you keeps you from envy, pride, rudeness and self-seeking behavior. It causes you to rejoice in the truth, to always have hope and always persevere (see 1 Cor. 13:4-7).

What does God require of you? *Generosity.* Knowing that He has given you all good things to enjoy, God wants you to live a generous life. Second Corinthians 9:7 tells us that God loves a cheerful giver. As Christ showed us, our giving is to be sacrificial and without expectation of repayment. Many times Jesus helped the poor, the crippled, the lame and the blind as an example for us to follow (see Luke 14:13-14). People with generous hearts eagerly look for such opportunities.

A Servant

Your wealth serves you—you don't serve it. Considering all that you are—an heir, worshiper and lover—the next logical step is to become a servant. It may not be exactly what you expected, because it sounds a little demeaning, but it's the greatest role a Christ-follower can have. Philippians 2:6-7 reminds us of the incredible sacrifice that Christ made in becoming a servant of mankind: "who, being in very nature God . . . made himself nothing, taking the very nature of a servant."

> Our problem is that any search for significance outside of Christ results in empty consumerism!

As a college student at Bethany College of Missions, I saw a living example of servanthood from the university president, Harold Brokke. Many students participated in a work-study program to help with their tuition. Some of those students worked in the cafeteria collecting and washing dishes. As I stood in line for lunch one day, I heard loud complaints coming from a student worker who clearly didn't like his job. It was the typical whining of someone who thought he shouldn't be expected to stoop so low as to wash dishes. Students were not allowed to choose their jobs; they were randomly assigned. This student obviously had a different job in mind that was more "worthy" of his talent, and he was letting everyone know about it.

I'll never forget what happened next. At the high point of the student's proclamation, Dr. Brokke put down his tray, took off his suit jacket, rolled up his sleeves, and walked over to the sink next to the whining student. Then, he simply took over the task of washing dishes.

I have never forgotten what I learned that day, and no lecture was required. I realized that serving means taking one's self out of the center of things and placing others first. I was also reminded of Jesus' example, when He took the lowly position as foot washer for the disciples. Hopefully, the student worker got it, too.

What does God require of you as a servant? Recognizing the incredible mercy and grace of God creates a life of humility. And humility produces a servant's heart. Instead of being in bondage to your possessions, your possessions should be used to serve others. James tells us it is hypocrisy to see a brother in need and simply "bless" him in the name of God, but do nothing to serve him (see Jas. 2:14-17). Humility destroys the pride of self-preservation and frees you to freely give.

God's Dream Is Greater

God is greater than the epidemic of materialism. His plans are greater than the American Dream. As a teenager, Nick Vujicic struggled with anger and questions over what his future would hold, even feeling as though God must have made a mistake with him. "God's got a plan for him, I can understand that. God's got a plan for her, I can understand that," Nick said. "But what's He going to do with me? What purpose is He going to fulfill through this? It just didn't make sense to me."

In our instant-gratification society, we don't like to wait, and we certainly don't like to be told no. But it wasn't until Nick learned to fully trust in God's sovereignty that he was able to find his purpose. Once Nick's focus was taken off his physical disability and struggles, God was able to begin using him to speak for

Him. "That's the great victory. When you can put your faith in God's grace, in God's plan, even when you don't understand."[12]

When you discover that your life can be hidden in Christ (see Col. 3:3), the power of selfishness is broken and replaced with godly contentment. You experience God's peace as you discover you're an heir with Christ, worshiper of God, lover and servant of others. In a world of consumers, you can know who you are and whose you are. And you can't buy that!

God, I give myself to You as a living sacrifice. Forgive me for adopting the behaviors of this world. I want to be a new person with fresh thoughts and actions, because I know only Your ways truly satisfy (see Rom. 12:1-2). Amen.

STUDY QUESTIONS

1. What is your most valuable possession?

2. What does conspicuous consumption mean?

3. What does the Bible say about our needs and consumption?

4. Have you ever experienced a robbery or break-in?

5. What's on your "If only" list?

6. Can you trust in God's sovereignty even when His answer is "no"? Why or why not?

7. Why is it so hard to live as a humble servant?

8. What would an honest inventory of your beliefs and your level of materialism look like on a balance sheet? How would they compare?

10

Now What?

By Joni Eareckson Tada

Imagine the emotions that must have welled up in the hearts of those who watched Jesus' ascension into heaven. Their hopes of an earthly kingdom, where justice would reign, seemed all but lost. Perhaps they looked at one another as if to say, "Now what?" We know that at least 120 of them gathered in the Upper Room to wait and pray for the Holy Spirit, as Jesus had instructed. There were, no doubt, other observers who returned to their homes, shaking their heads, and for them little changed. But when a chosen band of disciples, who are remembered as The Twelve, asked, "Now what?"—they changed the world! At the end of this study, we find ourselves at such a crossroads.

When people visit the Joni and Friends International Disability Center, one of the first things they see is a long gallery where many of my original paintings are on display. I love painting, even though I must hold the brushes between my teeth. Lately, I've noticed it's getting harder. Not just on my teeth, but my eyes. The other day I was signing limited-edition prints and, with my face so close to the drawing, I realized my reading glasses weren't enough—after signing 35 prints, everything looked blurry. That's when I put on my heavy-duty, industrial

> *Justice is a temporary thing that must at last come to an end;*
> *but the conscience is eternal and will never die.*
>
> Martin Luther (1483–1546)

> *'Tis nothing for a man to hold up his head in a calm; but to main-*
> *tain his post when all others have quitted their ground and they're*
> *to stand upright when other men are beaten down, is divine.*
>
> Seneca (AD 40–69)

strength, "thick as a nerd would wear" glasses. The lenses on these magnifying glasses are so thick, they hurt the bridge of my nose; but at least I am able to see clearly. My focus is sharpened and I can see the full picture.

For you, I imagine this Bible study has been a way of putting on heavy-duty glasses. I hope you can now see some of these complex issues more clearly—even more than others might. It's called vision, and it's what happens when we see the world as God pictures it.

God has a vision. He has a specific idea of what He wants this world to look like. It's a world where His justice and mercy reign (see Mic. 6:8), where His righteousness exalts nations (see Prov. 14:34), where the life and dignity of every human being is safeguarded (see Ps. 82:3-4), and where people live in peace (see Heb. 12:14). God's kingdom is one of righteousness, joy and peace (see Rom. 14:17), and Jesus references this in the prayer He taught His disciples: "Our Father in heaven, hallowed be your name, *your kingdom come, your will be done on earth as it is in heaven*" (Matt. 6:9-10, emphasis added). Every time we pray the Lord's Prayer, we are asking God to make the kingdom of Christ visible on earth. We are asking, "Lord, may Your kingdom of righteousness, justice and peace come, and may Your will be done here on earth exactly as You envision it in heaven . . . and give me the privilege of helping to make it happen!" It's what vision is all about—not only seeing the world as God pictures it, but helping to bring that picture into focus and make it *real*.

As a Christian, you are an ambassador for the kingdom of Christ. You are to make His kingdom *real* in a world currently occupied by the enemy; reclaiming earth as rightfully the King's. Your goal is to *proclaim* the gospel message as well as to *portray* it. In a world of injustice, pain and poverty, you are to reflect His justice, mercy and love.

And be encouraged! The adversary, who usurped God's authority in the Garden of Eden, knows his days are numbered. Although Satan enslaved the citizens of earth through treachery and deceit and set up his own rival government (see 1 John 5:19), he was dealt a mortal blow when Christ rose from the grave. Sin's power was canceled and Christ's kingdom is firmly established on "enemy territory" (see Matt. 11:12; Acts 26:18; Heb. 2:14; Rev. 1:18). You and I have the high privilege of freeing captive subjects and retaking earth under the Family banner. You and I are out to repossess this planet under the rightful Ruler, and every time we advance the gospel, we are "taking back" territory—not to mention people—that the enemy assumed were his. And we will continue to do so until "The kingdoms of this world are become the kingdoms of our Lord, and of his Christ; and he shall reign forever and ever" (Rev. 11:15, *KJV*).

Find Personal Balance in Life

Every solid study of Scripture should lead to the question, "Now what?" Even Scripture says, "Do not merely listen to the word, and so deceive yourselves. Do what it says" (Jas. 1:22). So you've listened, examined the Scriptures and discussed the issues. Now, what will you do with all that you've learned? How will it change your thoughts and actions? What about your conversations with your neighbors and friends? How will it influence your prayer and worship?

Your passion may not be one of the eight topics we've studied. You may have a heart for people with addictions, or you may feel drawn to help homeless families. You may be especially interested in the plight of seniors, or you may want to work against human trafficking or child abuse. You may feel led to help alleviate poverty or reverse the trend of illiteracy. The fact that you feel *led* to make a difference shows you have tapped deep into God's heart of compassion.

God's heart breaks for all those who suffer under the weight of pain and injustice. And, although skeptics will blame God for the world's sufferings, make no mistake: The Lord is bending over backward to alleviate the suffering. Psalm 10:17 makes God's intentions clear: "You hear, O LORD, the desire of the afflicted; you encourage them, and you listen to their cry, defending the fatherless and the oppressed." Our wonderful God is doing everything from His end to right what is wrong. But

He requires *us* to partner with Him to rescue the fragile, stop abortions, console the dying, minister to orphans, comfort the despairing, heal marriages, halt addictions and bind up the wounds of the brokenhearted. We can be a friend who speaks up on behalf of those who are too weak, too small or too old to speak for themselves.

As members of Christ's Body, we are His visible and present hands on earth, making "the kingdoms of this world become the kingdoms of our Lord." God uses our hands, time, treasure and talents to do His work in the world. Our Christian advocacy and service are part of our Christian witness. When it comes to proclaiming and portraying the gospel, advocacy can be considered part of "proclaiming" the gospel (declaring the good news), and service is "portraying" the gospel (demonstrating the good news). We cannot only preach the gospel; people must experience it. When we give the good news that Jesus Christ has come to redeem sinful man, we should show how it makes a difference. "Giving Christ" is always a picture of Christianity with its sleeves rolled up.

And rubber-meets-the-road Christianity involves being an advocate. Being an advocate means working for justice and mercy among the weakest and most vulnerable—not just in church communities but also in all of society (see Gal. 6:10). Here are some practical steps to becoming an advocate:

- *Look Around*—Hurting and needy people are in your own community. Once we are aware of their plight, we can no longer claim ignorance or remain blind to solutions. Consider the many people trapped in injustice and abuse overseas. Once, when my husband and I were visiting Thailand, we were enthralled with the beautiful beaches, but then someone showed us we were oblivious to the scores of brothels offering sex with adolescents just two blocks from the seashore. With our eyes opened, we were able to research and locate Christian organizations rescuing children from human trafficking.

- *Pray*—Pray against the temptation to despair when you move among the people and the families who are locked in the grip of injustice, poverty, abuse, old age or disability. I still struggle against feelings of discouragement when I help deliver wheelchairs overseas. The desperate plight of disabled children in less-developed nations is heartbreaking, and the needs are so *great!* Ask God to cultivate a love for the hurting people who are in circumstances unfamiliar to you—disability can be unpleasant, as well as homelessness and poverty. We must learn to look past the exterior and embrace the person who needs our help. Ask God to keep you from a spirit of bitterness as you relate to the perpetrators of abusive situations. Remember, you are not only representing Christ to those who are hurt, but to those who are part of the cycle of injustice, trafficking, abuse and poverty.

- *Pray for others*—It has been said that prayer does not fit us for the work of the Kingdom; prayer *is* the work of the Kingdom. God transforms communities, as well as the people who live in them, through the power of the prayers of His people. Prayer is the most influential form of advocacy. Through prayer, God changes the hearts and minds of people who, otherwise, would remain blind and indifferent to the injustices in our world. Ask God to enlarge your heart of compassion and for the courage to uphold those who are weak.

• *Learn More*—Connect with groups like the National Right to Life, the National Down Syndrome Congress, or the Center for Bioethics and Human Dignity. Find out what policies are encroaching on the welfare of disabled or elderly people, the unborn or newborn with disabilities. Do a Google search for contact information on these and other national organizations in fields that interest you. Find out what events or activities these groups are holding in your region—gather interested friends, sign up and participate!

• *Speak Up*—People in your church and in your community may be "deaf and blind" to the prevalence of violence, or to nursing home abuse, the plight of families with disabled children, the needs of the homeless, the suicide rate among young people, human trafficking in the city, or the assault on human life in research labs. The first principle of advocacy is to simply make your convictions known. Whether in conversations by the water cooler or in a coffee klatch, in a hair salon or during choir rehearsal, God asks us to share our views on the dignity of all human life. Journalist George Will once said that culture is like a giant slab of molasses, and voicing our convictions serve as tiny channels, guiding its lumbering movement.

• *Speak Out*—When you share your convictions, do so remembering that you are speaking on behalf of Jesus Christ. What good is it if we win the battle but lose people's souls in the process? Graciousness and gentleness of speech always win the day. The apostle Paul, the greatest defender of the faith, wrote, "Be wise in the way you act toward outsiders; make the most of every opportunity. Let your conversation be always full of grace, seasoned with salt, so that you may know how to answer everyone" (Col. 4:5-6). Finally, he advises Timothy to "Set an example for the believers in speech, in life, in love, in faith and in purity" (1 Tim. 4:12).

• *Empower Others*—Get to know, one on one, the very people about whom you feel passionate. Every advocate knows how important it is to stay connected to the people they serve. Often, those for whom we are advocating do not know the hope and help that is available in Jesus Christ. The art of advocacy is relationship building. Nothing is more rewarding than to witness a family or an individual rise above their circumstances to find hope in Christ. Facilitate a support group in your church for those families and individuals. Once empowered, those families may well be the best "spokespersons" for effecting change in peoples' hearts and transformation in a community.

• *Educate Others*—Coordinate a network of like-minded believers who will join you in your efforts to make a change in your community. Ask your pastor for permission to address your adult Sunday School on an issue you feel passionate about. Enlist the support of writers who can submit op-ed articles and letters to editors in your local newspaper. Do not tolerate irresponsibility in the media. When newspapers or television present a one-sided view on a critical issue, hold them accountable. When the media presents a slanted, incomplete or inaccurate portrayal of an issue involving the sanctity of life or justice, write to the newspaper editor or television station managers.

Create a small "watchdog" group to investigate bills and initiatives before your state assembly. For current information on legislative issues, contact the office of your state representative. Find out how your U.S. senators and congressional representatives in Washington, D.C., stand on issues. All politics is local, so remember to contact your senators or representative at their district offices (look in your phonebook for these addresses). Leverage your opinion by asking a few of your friends to call or write, and follow up by contacting your senators and representative at their Washington, D.C., address.

Balancing Faith and Culture

Do you feel ill-equipped or unskilled to lead on these issues? Do you feel that others are more qualified for the task? Not to worry. God delights in handpicking people for leadership who are ill-equipped for the mission. Now, if I were God, I would probably pick the smartest men and women possible to be on my team—the Ph.Ds, the college professors and top corporate executives. Then I would draft millionaires to finance the work. My public relations people would be the most effective communicators to be found anywhere—tops in their field! To qualify even as a mere rank-and-file member of my advocacy team, a person would have to be knowledgeable, articulate, bright and attractive. Weak people need not apply.

Thank God I'm not running the world—He is. And He opens His arms to the weak and ungifted, the unlovely and unlikely. That's because of His great love (it's also because what's in a person's heart matters more to Him than what's on the outside, or how much training he has or how skilled a communicator he is).

If you feel unskilled to be a spokesperson on the issues we've studied, you're just the person God is looking for! Through your weakness, God will bring maximum glory to Himself. The apostle Paul told the Corinthian Christians to look around and realize that—on the whole—God had called people who, by human standards, were neither wise nor influential. He's saying that God deliberately chooses weak and limited candidates to get His work done so that when the job is accomplished, the glory goes to Him. In this way the gospel goes forth and the Kingdom is advanced in power and might (see 1 Cor. 1:26)!

Personally, when I first dived into disability advocacy, I was still struggling to adjust to my own wheelchair. I still felt funny around people with other conditions, like cerebral palsy or blindness. I had more of a "fear of man" than I did a "fear of God." When I finally got my feet wet in advocacy work, I had to forget everything I'd been taught about personal power leading to effective leadership. Confidence, charisma, and chutzpah count for little over the long haul. My friend Dr. Dan Allender has said that "the leaders God chooses are more broken than strong; more damaged than whole; more troubled than secure. The most effective leaders don't rise to power in spite of their weakness; they lead with power because of their weakness."[1]

Look closely and you'll discover that Jesus, our Advocate, led with power because of His weakness and humility. If you study the life of the world's greatest leader—Jesus Christ—you learn two things: He was a visionary; that is, He could set a course for His followers and move forward with unflinching confidence. Yet at the same time, He was a servant who got down on His hands and knees and washed the feet of His disciples. Jesus led by casting the vision (advocacy), then He modeled the vision (serving), empowering and supporting everyone around Him.

For example, Jesus cast the vision in Luke 14:12-14 as He said, "When you give a luncheon or dinner, do not invite your friends, your brothers or relatives, or your rich neighbors . . . but when you give a banquet, invite the poor, the crippled, the lame, the blind." Then He flipped the coin and modeled that vision, so much so, that it irked His disciples who expected Him to "act like a real Messiah should act." Once, He and His disciples, along with a crowd of tagalongs, were leaving Jericho on ministry business when Jesus stopped for a blind man. The disciples were nearly outraged (see Mark 10:46-52). As hundreds looked on, the most important prophet to come along in centuries stooped to serve a blind beggar! But in doing so, Jesus modeled a true vision of advocacy and service for us all. From then on, His disciples probably never looked at a blind man the same. Mission accomplished . . . through servant-leadership!

So don't be worried about what others think or what the experts say. You have God Himself defending you to the so-called experts, for He says, "Where is the wise man? Where is the scholar? Where is the philosopher [the so-called ethicist] of this age? Has not God made foolish the wisdom of the world? . . . God chose the foolish things of the world to shame the wise; God chose the weak things of the world to shame the strong" (1 Cor. 1:20,27). Keep boasting in the strength and knowledge of the Lord, and you can't go wrong. Luke 12:11-12 assures, "Do not worry about how you will defend yourselves or what you will say, *for the Holy Spirit will teach you at that time what you should say*" (emphasis added).

Heroes of the faith (all of them unlikely candidates) have *always* addressed the kinds of issues we've been examining. The great Christian William Wilberforce campaigned for years to successfully defeat slave trade laws in Great Britain. And look at all the modern-day heroes who have started movements: Kay Warren was transformed from living a comfortable middle-class life, as Pastor Rick Warren's wife, to becoming active in the church's global response to the HIV/AIDS pandemic. Chuck Colson, after his indictment and incarceration from the Nixon-Watergate scandal, rose to lead a worldwide movement of social justice and prison reform. And Nancy Leigh DeMoss, a young single woman, has ignited a nationwide movement to revive the biblical view of womanhood.

Heroes of the faith not only present the message of salvation, but they also help people experience salvation. You've met some of these heroes in this study. They are ordinary, everyday people who are not merely caught up in a cause . . . they are captivated by Christ. And they are making Him real in our world.

Culture Reflects What We Worship

The *most important* change has to do with heart. Our nation needs heart—a moral center, renewed and inspired. The genuine rights of the weak, the disadvantaged, the unborn, the child, the elderly and even the cloned can only be safeguarded in a society that honors life, treats humanity with respect and shows heart. The Lord speaks to this lack of heart in Deuteronomy 30:16-20: "I command you today to love the LORD your God, to walk in his ways, and to keep his commands, decrees and laws; then you will live and increase, and the LORD your God will bless you in the land you are entering to possess. But *if your heart turns away and you are not obedient* . . . I declare to you this day that you will certainly be destroyed. You will not live long in the land you are crossing the Jordan to enter and possess" (emphasis added).

I know a little bit about heart and advocacy. As I said earlier, under the presidencies of Ronald Reagan and George H. W. Bush, I was appointed to the National Council on Disability. It was our responsibility to advise these two administrations, as well as Congress, on disability-related issues. I will never forget sitting on the White House lawn with other council members in the spring of 1990, as President Bush signed the Americans with Disabilities Act into law. It was a great day. This new legislation was designed to remove discrimination and provide access to employment, public buildings and transportation. After the signing ceremony, our council members went to a nearby hotel for a reception. As champagne was passed around, our council's executive director, Paul Hearne, seemed quiet. After fingering his glass, he said he'd like to make an announcement.

"This new law will mean there will soon be mechanical lifts on buses," he said, "and ramps into restaurants . . . and open doors in places of employment." Paul then fell silent. After a long moment, he continued, "But this law will not change the heart of the bus driver. It will not change the heart of the restaurant owner or the employer." Then with wet eyes, he lifted his glass in a toast and said, "Here's to changed hearts."

Suddenly, I couldn't stop the tears. They flowed freely and unashamedly as I realized, *That's the job of the Church. That's our responsibility. We have the message that can actually change people's hearts!* Civil rights legislation, public policy and state proclamations will not and cannot transform the heart. Only the gospel of Jesus Christ can do that. Education and public policy can inform, but not transform, individuals and the societies in which they live. Culture is a reflection of what we worship, and if we want to change our culture, it must mean introducing people to the one and only true God who deserves our worship.

God tells us in Ezekiel 11:19-20, "I will remove from them their heart of stone and give them a heart of flesh. Then they will follow my decrees and be careful to keep my laws. They will be my people, and I will be their God." I don't want America to move into the future with a heart of stone. Christians are charged with the only message that can transform the heart of the bus driver, restaurant owner and employer. We are commissioned to shake gospel salt and shine gospel light at the market and dry cleaners, at PTA meetings or in university classrooms. We have the message, the gospel of Jesus Christ, and God has given us the means to speak to the secularists who promote the idea that everyone should be free to do what is right in his or her own eyes (see Judg. 21:25). If advocacy means building relationships, then it requires sharing Christ one on one. One person at a time—it is at *this fundamental level* that a nation's heart is transformed.

It's how my heart was healed when, after I was first injured, I despaired of life as a quadriplegic. Although I knew Christ as Lord and Savior, doubts and fear were quickly eroding my faith. I needed to see Jesus "with skin on." I needed to be assured that my life was not spinning out of control into nightmarish chaos. Thank God He sent His advocates my way. They were Christian friends and visitors, neighbors and family members who demonstrated to me the heart of Christ. They came into the hospital and rehab center where I was institutionalized for two years and made Jesus Christ *real* to me. Through prayer and Bible reading, they assured me God had a plan for my life. Plus, they spoke up for my needs and gave voice to my plight (and the needs of my roommates). They advocated for us, whether to the floor supervisor when our sheets were soiled and left unchanged, or at the University of Maryland where I needed access to second-story classrooms. These Christian friends were God's hands. They were His advocates for one depressed and paralyzed young girl, and I am still feeling the repercussions of their advocacy and loving service.

You are like these friends. Please never forget that in all your advocacy and service to the needy, the state of their souls trumps everything else. After all, what good does it do if wrongs are made right if people face an eternity without Jesus Christ? Make certain your Christian service doesn't become merely *social* service with no invitation for an individual or a family to open their hearts to the Savior. Yes, always "show" the Good News, but be sure to "tell" the salvation message, too.

For Such a Time as This!

"This is what the LORD says: 'Let not the wise man boast of his wisdom or the strong man boast of his strength . . . but let him who boasts boast about this: that he understands and knows me, that I am the LORD, who exercises kindness, justice and righteousness on earth, for in these I delight,' declares the LORD" (Jer. 9:23-24).

This is an exciting time in which to live! A time ripe with opportunity! Now is *not* the time to wag our finger at secularists and become irritable that humanists and left-leaning media have hijacked our society. Now is not the season to shrug our shoulders, step aside and let others draw the line in the sand. The battle cry has been sounded—a call to arms—and whether it's people like those we've met in our book, or those trapped in human trafficking, child or elder abuse, poverty or homelessness, we can courageously present the good news of Jesus. It is time to rise and "Speak up for those who cannot speak for themselves, for the rights of all who are destitute. Speak up and judge fairly; defend the rights of the poor and needy" (Prov. 31:8-9). It is a season like none other to show a skeptical, cynical world what a society looks like when Christ is exalted; when it honors life and treats all human beings, no matter what their condition, with respect. Things change when people get *that* engaged.

You can begin making a difference today by reading, reflecting on and then signing the Manhattan Declaration. It's not a statement of faith; it's a statement of conscience. As a Christian, you are an heir of a 2,000-year-old tradition of proclaiming God's Word, seeking justice, resisting tyranny and reaching out with compassion to the poor, oppressed and suffering. The Manhattan Declaration will give you "a line drawn in the sand" from which you need never flinch. It will inspire courage in your convictions, and it will unite you with hundreds of thousands of other Christians who are committed to the timeless biblical principles that make up the foundation of the Judeo-Christian ethic. A summary of the Manhattan Declaration is contained in this book. To review the entire document and add your signature, just visit manhattandeclaration.org.

Thank you for joining me and my friends in this important study! I hope you found it enlightening and encouraging to your faith. I consider it a privilege to stand alongside you, my friend, for you are an ambassador who represents God's kindness, justice and righteousness on earth. You have a message that will touch the hearts of individuals and the soul of this great nation. Because it really *is* all about Jesus!

Bring More of What I Dream
by Ted Loder

O God,
who out of nothing
brought everything that is,
out of what I am
bring more of what I dream

but haven't dared,
direct my power and passion
to creating life
where there is death,
to putting flesh of action
on bare-boned intentions,
to lighting fires
against the midnight of indifference,
to throwing bridges of care,
across canyons of loneliness,
so I can look on creation,
together with you,
and behold,
call it very good;
through Jesus Christ my Lord.[2]

STUDY QUESTIONS

1. Which topic in this study has sharpened your focus the most? Why?

2. What do you think God wants His world to look like?

3. Our goal as Christ's ambassadors is to proclaim the gospel message throughout the world. How are we doing?

4. How will this study change your thoughts and actions? Your conversations with neighbors and friends? How will it influence your prayer and worship?

5. What is Christian advocacy?

6. How can you know what God wants you to do to advocate for the weakest and most vulnerable in our society?

7. What did Joni mean when she said that if you feel unskilled to be a spokesperson on an issue, you're just the person God is looking for?

8. Our world needs a change of heart, a moral center and a godly vision. In what ways will you make Christ real in your community?

The Manhattan Declaration[1]

A Summary

Preamble

Christians are heirs of a 2,000-year tradition of proclaiming God's word, seeking justice in our societies, resisting tyranny, and reaching out with compassion to the poor, oppressed and suffering.

While fully acknowledging the imperfections and shortcomings of Christian institutions and communities in all ages, we claim the heritage of those Christians who defended innocent life by rescuing discarded babies from trash heaps in Roman cities and publicly denouncing the Empire's sanctioning of infanticide. We remember with reverence those believers who sacrificed their lives by remaining in Roman cities to tend the sick and dying during the plagues, and who died bravely in the coliseums rather than deny their Lord.

After the barbarian tribes overran Europe, Christian monasteries preserved not only the Bible but also the literature and art of Western culture. It was Christians who combated the evil of slavery: Papal edicts in the 16th and 17th centuries decried the practice of slavery and first excommunicated anyone involved in the slave trade; evangelical Christians in England, led by John Wesley and William Wilberforce, put an end to the slave trade in that country. Christians under Wilberforce's leadership also formed hundreds of societies for helping the poor, the imprisoned, and child laborers chained to machines.

In Europe, Christians challenged the divine claims of kings and successfully fought to establish the rule of law and balance of governmental powers, which made modern democracy possible. And in America, Christian women stood at the vanguard of the suffrage movement. The great civil rights crusades of the 1950s and '60s were led by Christians claiming the Scriptures and asserting the glory of the image of God in every human being regardless of race, religion, age or class.

This same devotion to human dignity has led Christians in recent decades to work to end the dehumanizing scourge of human trafficking and sexual slavery, bring compassionate care to AIDS sufferers in Africa, and assist in a myriad of other human rights causes—from providing clean water in developing nations to providing homes for tens of thousands of children orphaned by war, disease and gender discrimination.

Like those who have gone before us in the faith, Christians today are called to proclaim the Gospel of costly grace, to protect the intrinsic dignity of the human person and to stand for the common good. In being true to its own calling—the call to discipleship—the church through service to others can make a profound contribution to the public good.

The Declaration
Christians, when they have lived up to the highest ideals of their faith, have defended the weak and vulnerable and worked tirelessly to protect and strengthen vital institutions of civil society, beginning with the family.

We are Orthodox, Catholic, and evangelical Christians who have united at this hour to reaffirm fundamental truths about justice and the common good, and to call upon our fellow citizens, believers and non-believers alike, to join us in defending them. These truths are (1) the sanctity of human life, (2) the dignity of marriage as the conjugal union of husband and wife, and (3) the rights of conscience and religious liberty. Inasmuch as these truths are foundational to human dignity and the well-being of society, they are inviolable and non-negotiable. Because they are increasingly under assault from powerful forces in our culture, we are compelled today to speak out forcefully in their defense, and to commit ourselves to honoring them fully no matter what pressures are brought upon us and our institutions to abandon or compromise them. We make this commitment not as partisans of any political group but as followers of Jesus Christ, the crucified and risen Lord, who is the Way, the Truth, and the Life.

Human Life

The lives of the unborn, the disabled, and the elderly are ever more threatened. While public opinion has moved in a pro-life direction, powerful and determined forces are working to expand abortion, embryo-destructive research, assisted suicide, and euthanasia. Although the protection of the weak and vulnerable is the first obligation of government, the power of government is today often enlisted in the cause of promoting what Pope John Paul II called "the culture of death." We pledge to work unceasingly for the equal protection of every innocent human being at every stage of development and in every condition. We will refuse to permit ourselves or our institutions to be implicated in the taking of human life and we will support in every possible way those who, in conscience, take the same stand.

Marriage

The institution of marriage, already wounded by promiscuity, infidelity and divorce, is at risk of being redefined and thus subverted. Marriage is the original and most important institution for sustaining the health, education, and welfare of all. Where marriage erodes, social pathologies rise. The impulse to redefine marriage is a symptom, rather than the cause, of the erosion of the marriage culture. It reflects a loss of understanding of the meaning of marriage as embodied in our civil law as well as our religious traditions. Yet it is critical that the impulse be resisted, for yielding to it would mean abandoning the possibility of restoring a sound understanding of marriage and, with it, the hope of rebuilding a healthy marriage culture. It would lock into place the false and destructive belief that marriage is all about romance and other adult satisfactions, and more [than] not, in any intrinsic way, about the unique character and value of acts and relationships whose meaning is shaped by their aptness for the generation, promotion and protection of life. Marriage is not a "social construction," but is rather an objective reality—the covenantal union of husband and wife—that it is the duty of the law to recognize, honor, and protect.

Religious Liberty

Freedom of religion and the rights of conscience are gravely jeopardized. The threat to these fundamental principles of justice is evident in efforts to weaken or eliminate conscience protections for healthcare institutions and professionals, and in antidiscrimination statutes that are used as weapons to force religious institutions, charities, businesses, and service providers either to accept (and even facilitate) activities and relationships they judge to be immoral, or go out of business. Attacks on religious liberty are dire threats not only to individuals, but also to the institutions of civil society including families, charities, and religious communities. The health and wellbeing of such institutions provide an indispensable buffer against the overweening power of government and is essential to the flourishing of every other institution—including government itself—on which society depends.

Unjust Laws

As Christians, we believe in law, and we respect the authority of earthly rulers. We count it a special privilege to live in a democratic society where the moral claims of the law on us are even stronger in virtue of the rights of all citizens to participate in the political process. Yet even in a democratic regime, laws can be unjust. And from the beginning, our faith has taught that civil disobedience is required in the face of gravely unjust laws or laws that purport to require us to do what is unjust or otherwise immoral. Such laws lack the power to bind in conscience because they can claim no authority beyond that of sheer human will.

Therefore, let it be known that we will not comply with any edict that compels us or the institutions we lead to participate in or facilitate abortions, embryo-destructive research, assisted suicide, euthanasia, or any other act that violates the principle of the profound, inherent and equal dignity of every member of the human family.

Further, let it be known that we will not bend to any rule forcing us to bless immoral sexual partnerships, treat them as marriages or the equivalent or refrain from proclaiming the truth, as we know it, about morality, marriage and the family.

Further, let it be known that we will not be intimidated into silence or acquiescence or the violation of our consciences by any power on earth, be it cultural or political, regardless of the consequences to ourselves. We will fully and ungrudgingly render to Caesar what is Caesar's. But under no circumstances will we render to Caesar what is God's.

Drafting Committee
Robert George, Professor, McCormick Professor of Jurisprudence, Princeton University

Timothy George, Professor, Beeson Divinity School, Samford University

Chuck Colson, Founder, the Chuck Colson Center for Christian Worldview (Lansdowne, VA)

Appendix B

Glossary of Terminology

Following are some brief definitions of terms used in this book regarding disabilities and bioethics.

advance directive: instructions given by an individual specifying what actions should be taken for their health in the event that they are no longer able to make decisions due to illness or incapacity.

Alzheimer's disease: a progressive neurological disease of the brain that leads to irreversible loss of neurons, and dementia. Clinical hallmarks are progressive memory impairment, judgment, decision-making, orientation to surroundings and language. Diagnosis made on the basis of a neurologic examination, but a definitive diagnosis can only be made at autopsy.

Asperger's syndrome: an autistic disorder most notable for a discrepancy between intellectual and social abilities. Typical features may include uncoordinated motor movements, social impairment with extreme egocentricity, limited interests, topical preoccupations and expertise, repetitive routines or rituals, speech and language peculiarities and nonverbal communication problems. Sometimes referred to as high-functioning autism.

autism: a complex developmental disability that typically appears during the first three years of life and is the result of a neurological disorder that affects the normal functioning of the brain, impacting development in the areas of social interaction, communication skills and sensory integration. Both children and adults with autism typically show difficulties in verbal and nonverbal communication, social interactions and leisure or play activities.

Autism Spectrum Disorders: a range of neurological disorders that most markedly involve some degree of difficulty with communication and interpersonal relationships, as well as obsessions and repetitive behaviors, ranging from lower to higher functioning. Diagnoses include autism, Asperger's syndrome, Rett syndrome, childhood disintegrative disorder and pervasive developmental disorder.

behavior modification: usually a one-on-one intensive, structured teaching program for children with autism spectrum disorder or other disabilities, using reinforced practice of different skills. Can be called applied behavior analysis, discrete trial therapy, functional communication training, incidental teaching, behavior chaining or errorless learning, among others.

bioethicist: a person who studies the ethical and moral implications of new biological discoveries and biomedical advances.

cerebral palsy: a term used to describe a group of chronic conditions affecting body movements and muscle coordination. It is caused by damage to one or more specific areas of the brain, usually occurring during fetal development or infancy. It can also occur before, during or shortly following birth.

developmental disabilities: severe, chronic disabilities attributed to mental or physical impairments (or a combination of the two) occurring before adulthood and resulting in substantial functional limitations in major life activities. Examples include autism, cerebral palsy, Down syndrome, mental retardation and spina bifida.

Down syndrome: also called trisomy 21, is caused by the presence of all or part of an extra twenty-first chromosome. It is characterized by a combination of major and minor differences in structure, a particular set of facial characteristics and is often associated with some impairment of cognitive ability, ranging from mild to severe developmental disabilities.

eugenics: the study of or belief in the possibility of improving the qualities of the human species or a human population, especially by such means as discouraging reproduction by persons having genetic defects or presumed to have inheritable undesirable traits (negative eugenics), or encouraging reproduction by persons presumed to have inheritable desirable traits (positive eugenics).

euthanasia: the act of putting to death, or allowing to die, a person with an incurable or painful disease or condition by withholding extreme medical measures or by administering a lethal dose of medication.

genocide: the deliberate and systematic extermination of a national, racial, political, religious or cultural group.

germline: the sequence of cells that develop into eggs and sperm. Also, inherited material that comes from the eggs or sperm and is passed on to offspring.

health care proxy: designation of a surrogate medical decision-maker in the event that a person becomes unable to make medical decisions on his own behalf.

juvenile arthritis: rheumatoid arthritis is the most common type of arthritis in children under the age of 16 and causes persistent joint pain, swelling and stiffness. Symptoms can appear for a few months or for a lifetime. Some types of juvenile rheumatoid arthritis can cause serious complications, such as growth problems and eye inflammation. Treatment focuses on controlling pain, improving function and preventing joint damage.

Manhattan Declaration: a 4,700-word declaration speaking in defense of the sanctity of life, traditional marriage and religious liberty, released on November 20, 2009, by a group of prominent Christian clergy, ministry leaders and scholars. It issues a call to Christians to adhere firmly to their convictions in these areas. (See appendix A for a summary, or read the entire document at http://manhattandeclaration.org/read.aspx.)

materialism: a preoccupation with or emphasis on material objects, comforts and considerations, with a disinterest in or rejection of spiritual, intellectual or cultural values.

multiple sclerosis (MS): a disease of the central nervous system marked by numbness, weakness, loss of muscle coordination and problems with vision, speech and bladder control. MS is an autoimmune disease in which the body's immune system attacks myelin, a key substance that serves as a nerve insulator and helps in the transmission of nerve signals. The progress, severity and specific symptoms in MS are unpredictable. One never knows when attacks will occur, how long they will last or how severe they will be.

muscular dystrophy (MD): a term used to describe a number of inherited disorders characterized by progressive weakness and wasting of the muscles. The most common and severe type is Duchenne's MD, in which a genetic defect leads to the formation of an abnormal type of muscle protein called dystrophin and is progressive and terminal.

Parkinson's disease: a slowly progressive neurologic disease characterized by a fixed, inexpressive face, tremor while resting, slowing of voluntary movements, a gait with short, accelerating steps, peculiar posture and muscle weakness, all caused by a degeneration of an area of the brain called the basal ganglia and by low production of the neurotransmitter dopamine.

pervasive developmental disorder (PDD): a category of neurological disorders characterized by severe and pervasive impairment in several areas of development and included as an autism spectrum disorder.

picture exchange communication system (PECs): a form of augmentative and alternate communication that uses pictures instead of words to help children communicate. PECs was designed especially for children with autism who have delays in speech development.

pre-implantation genetic diagnosis (PGD): a procedure used in conjunction with in vitro fertilization to screen for specific genetic or chromosomal abnormalities, or gender, before transferring the fertilized eggs into the mother.

quadriplegic: a person who is paralyzed, with partial or total loss of use of legs, arms and torso, with both sensation and control of movement being affected.

Rett syndrome: an inherited developmental disorder, usually observed only in females, that is characterized by a short period of normal development, followed by loss of developmental skills (particularly purposeful hand movements) and marked psychomotor retardation. A brief autistic-like phase may be observed during the preschool period, but the subsequent course and clinical features are markedly different from autism, although it is included as an autism spectrum disorder.

ritualistic behaviors: restricted, repetitive and stereotyped behaviors, which present themselves as obsessive interests, rigid adherence to routines, stereotyped motor movements and preoccupation with parts of or whole objects.

sensory integration: a neurological process that organizes sensation from one's own body and the environment, making it possible to make sense of the environment. Children with autism have trouble learning to do this, with some senses being excessively hypersensitive and others hyposensitive. Sensory integration therapy is a form of occupational therapy that is specifically designed to stimulate and challenge all of the senses to work together.

social scripts: (also known as social stories) an intervention strategy to help teach children with autism spectrum disorder self-awareness, self-calming and self-management skills. Usually written with the child, they target social situations that are difficult for the child to navigate and tell a story from beginning to end with desired outcome. Creating, reading and practicing a social script can help a child learn how to achieve that desired outcome.

spectrum disorder: a group of disorders with similar features and causation, ranging from mild to severe symptoms.

spina bifida: a congenital malformation (present at birth) in which there is a bony defect in the vertebral column so that part of the spinal cord is exposed. People with spina bifida can have bladder and bowel incontinence, cognitive and learning problems and limited mobility.

stem cell: a cell that, upon division, replaces its own numbers and also gives rise to cells that differentiate further into one or more specialized types—a "master" or "blank slate" cell that is very pliable and has the ability to change into almost any other kind of body tissue. Stem cells can be retrieved from adult tissues or human embryos.

utilitarianism: the doctrine that virtue is based on utility and that conduct should be directed toward promoting the greatest good and happiness for the greatest number of persons, while sacrificing the weak and vulnerable in order to do so.

Zellweger syndrome: an inherited condition that damages the white matter of the brain and also affects how the body metabolizes particular substances in the blood and organ tissues, causing neurological abnormalities, facial deformities and lack of muscle tone among other problems. There is no cure and no treatment. Most will die by six months of age.

Appendix C

Recommended Resources

*From Joni and Friends International
Disability Center*

Books

A Lifetime of Wisdom: Embracing the Way God Heals You by Joni Eareckson Tada (2009)

Autism and Your Church: Nurturing the Spiritual Growth of People with Autism Spectrum Disorder by Barbara J. Newman (2006)

Finding Your Child's Way on the Autism Spectrum: Discovering Unique Strengths, Mastering Behavior Challenges by Dr. Laura Hendrickson (2009)

How to Be a Christian in a Brave New World by Dr. Nigel Cameron and Joni Eareckson Tada (2006)

Special Needs Smart Pages, Advice, Answers and Articles about Ministering to Children with Special Needs by Joni and Friends (2009)

When God Weeps: Why Our Sufferings Matter to the Almighty by Joni Eareckson Tada and Steve Estes (1997)

Joni and Friends TV Series

Hosted by Joni Eareckson Tada

I've Got Questions: Featuring Nick Vujicic (DVDTV08)

Holding on to Hope: Featuring David and Nancy Guthrie (DVDTV11)

Holly's Heart: Featuring Holly Strother (DVDTV21)

Lives in the Balance: The Stem Cell Debate: Featuring Laura
Dominquez (DVDTV22)
Making Sense of Autism: Part 1 and Part 2 (DVDTV30)
The Terri Schiavo Story: Two-part Episode (DVDTV18)
When Robin Prays: Featuring Robin Hiser (DVDTV05)
When Life Isn't Fair: Featuring Vicky Olivas (DVDTV07)

Websites

Ability Online: www.ablelink.org
Americans United for Life: www.aul.org
American Values: www.ouramericanvalues.org
Autism Speaks: www.autismspeaks.org
Autism Society: www.autismsociety.org
Child Help: www.childhelp.org
CLC Network: www.clcnetwork.org
Counsel of Biotechpolicy: www.biotechpolocy.org
Crown Financial Ministry: www.crown.org
Family Research Center: www.frc.org
Friendship Ministries: www.friendship.org
Institute in Basic Life Principles: www.iblp.org
National Autism Association: www.nationalautismassociation.org
SaveOne: www.saveone.org

Joni and Friends International Disability Center

www.joniandfriends.org
P.O. Box 3333, Agoura Hills, CA 91376
(818) 707-5664 TTY (818) 707-9707

Appendix D

Joni and Friends International Disability Center

Joni Eareckson Tada is the founder of the Joni and Friends International Disability Ministry and an advocate for the disability community that numbers 660 million people worldwide.

Our Mission is to communicate the gospel and equip Christ-honoring churches worldwide to evangelize and disciple people affected by disabilities. In doing this:

- We present the clear and concise gospel of Jesus Christ to all people with disabilities and their families served through our programs.
- We train, disciple and mentor people affected by disability to exercise their gifts of leadership and service in the church and their communities.
- We energize the church to move from lack of awareness to including persons with disabilities into the fabric of worship, fellowship and outreach.

The Christian Institute on Disability

Leaders in the church and community have long looked to Joni Eareckson Tada and Joni and Friends as an authoritative Christian voice on critical issues of disability. To carry the work of education and advocacy to the next level, the Joni and Friends International Disability Center has established the Christian Institute on Disability to aggressively promote a Christ-centered, biblical approach that protects human dignity and the sanctity of all human life, no matter what the disabling condition.

The mission of the Christian Institute on Disability is to impact the church, Christian and public institutions and societies with a biblical worldview and life-giving truth on issues pertaining to life, dignity, justice and equality that affect people with disabilities. This mission is carried out through education programs in churches, colleges and seminaries.

Beyond Suffering: Christian Views on Disability Ministry, the 32-hour Certificate in Disability Ministry awarded by the Christian Institute on Disability, is designed to give participants an introductory understanding of the aspects of disabilities. *Beyond Suffering* is comprised of four thought-provoking modules: Overview of Disability, Theology of Disability, Church and Disability, and Introduction to Bioethics. Participants will learn through lecture, group discussion, video and hands-on experience how to evangelize and empower those affected by disability. This program is designed for ministers, professionals, teachers, volunteers, students and anyone interested in learning more about effective disability ministry. See www.joniandfriends.org/CID.

Download Public Policy Papers

These position papers are copyrighted and available for you to download and copy freely, without changing or adding to the information:

09 Revised JAF position on ESC
Policy Center Guidelines
Postmodernism
Stem Cell Research White Paper
McReynolds Response Article
Stem Cell Research
A Knowledge Tradition
From Whence Comes Rights
Language Disability
Luke and A Theology of Suffering and Disability
Prenatal Genetic Testing
Why Christian Doctrine Matters

www.joniandfriends.org/christian-institute-on-disability

Endnotes

Chapter 1: Life's Sticky Dilemma

1. Conversation with Doug Mazza, 2009.
2. Dictionary.com, based on the *Random House Dictionary*, © Random House, Inc. 2010, s.v. "abortion." http://dictionary.reference.com/browse/abortion.
3. A similar statement can be attributed to political commentator George Will.
4. Susan W. Enouen, PE, "Down Syndrome and Abortion," *Physicians for Life*, 2010.
5. Gordon R. Preece, *Rethinking Peter Singer: A Christian Critique* (Downer's Grove, IL: InterVarsity Press, 2002), p. 49.
6. George Washington, "Washington's Farewell Address 1796," quoted at the Lillian Goldman Law Library of the Yale Law School. http://avalon.law.yale.edu/18th_century/washing.asp.
7. "Economic Materialism," Wikipedia.org. http://en.wikipedia.org/wiki/Economic_materialism.

Chapter 2: When Life Isn't Fair: Violence in the Streets

1. Bryan Robinson, "Convicted Killer of Ennis Cosby Confesses: Convicted Killer Apologizes and Withdraws Appeal," ABC News, February 9, 2010. http://abcnews.go.com/US/story?id=94100&page=1.
2. Rosalind Rossi and Art Golab, "I Can't Go Outside," *Chicago Sun-Times*, August 6, 2008. http://www.suntimes.com/news/education/1093215,CST-NWS-prisoner06.article
3. "Statistics," Rape Abuse and Incest National Network, 2009. http://www.rainn.org/statistics.
4. "Gang Statistics," Helping Gang Youth, 2009. http://www.helpinggangyouth.com/statistics.html.
5. "National Child Abuse Statistics," Childhelp, 2007. http://www.childhelp.org/resources/learning-center/statistics.
6. Matthew R. Durose et al., U.S. Department of Justice, NCJ 207846, Bureau of Justice Statistics, "Family Violence Statistics: Including Statistics on Strangers and Acquaintances, at 31-32 (2005)," http://www.ojp.usdoj.gov/bjs/pub/pdf/fvs.pdf.
7. Richard J. Bonnie and Robert B. Wallace, eds., Committee on National Statistics and Behavioral and Social Sciences and Education, "Elder Mistreatment: Abuse, Neglect and Exploitation in an Aging America," 2003. http://www.nap.edu/openbook.php?isbn=0309084342.
8. "School Crime Victimization," Office of Justice Programs, Office of Juvenile Justice and Delinquency Prevention, 2006. http://ojjdp.ncjrs.gov/ojstatbb/victims/qa02201.asp?qaDate=2006.
9. D. Sobsey, D. Wells, R. Lucardie and S. Mansell, *Violence and Disability: An Annotated Bibliography* (Baltimore, MD: Brookes Publishing, 1995). http://www.avhotline.org/abuse/statistics/index.html#elder.
10. "National Child Abuse Statistics," Childhelp, 2007. http://www.childhelp.org/resources/learning-center/statistics.
11. David Powlison, *Anger: Escaping the Maze*, Resources for Changing Lives, The Christian Counseling Education Foundation (Phillipsburg, NJ: P&R Publishing, 2000), p. 3.
12. The ideas in this section are borrowed from Bill Gothard's "Institute in Basic Youth Conflicts," *Research in Principles of Life* (Oak Brook, IL: 1971).

Chapter 3: Making Sense of Autism

1. Mary Sanchez, "Evolution of Our Awareness of Mental Health," *Kansas City Star/Dallas Morning News,* February 15, 2010, p. 15A.

2. "What Is Autism? Facts and Stats," Autism Society, 2003. www. http://www.educa tion.com/reference/article/Ref_What_Autism_Facts/.

3. Ibid.

4. Francis Chan, *Crazy Love* (Colorado Springs, CO: David C. Cook Ministries, 2008), p. 25.

5. *Making Sense of Autism: Part 1 and 2,* Joni and Friends TV episodes, DVDTV30.

6. Ibid.

7. Ibid.

8. Ibid.

9. Sarah Stup, quoted in Aaron Notarianni Stephens, "Silent Echoes," *Exceptional Parents,* October 2008, vol. 38, no. 10, p. 25.

10. G.L.U.E. Team is a trademark of CLC Network, www.clcnetwork.org.

11. Joni and Friends, "Outreach: Creating a G.L.U.E. Team" *Special Needs Smart Pages* (Ventura, CA: Gospel Light, 2009), pp. 139-141.

12. *Making Sense of Autism: Part 2,* Joni and Friends TV episodes, DVDTV30.

13. Molly Kantz, "My Brother Willson," cited in Joni and Friends, *Special Needs Smart Pages,* pp. 261-262.

14. *Making Sense of Autism: Part 2,* Joni and Friends TV episodes, DVDTV30.

15. Dr. Laura Hendrickson, *Finding Your Child's Way on the Autism Spectrum* (Chicago: Moody Publishers, 2009), p. 128.

16. Joni Eareckson Tada, *More Precious Than Silver* (Grand Rapids, MI: Zondervan Publishing House, 1998). Used by permission.

17. Chan, *Crazy Love,* p. 26.

Chapter 4: Self-Image in a Fickle Culture

1. "A Senate Chaplain's Self-Image," *Christianity Today,* June 2008. http://www.christianity today.com/moi/2008/003/june/20.20.html.

2. T.R. Nansel, M. Overpeck, R.S. Pilla, et al, "Bullying Behaviors Among US Youth: Preva-lence and Association with Psychosocial Adjustment," *The Journal of the American Medical Association,* 2001, vol. 285, no. 16, pp. 2094-2100.

3. Sharon Jaynes, *The Power of a Woman's Words* (Eugene, OR: Harvest House Publishers, 2007), pp. 50-52.

4. Visit the Institute in Basic Life Principles, a biblically based, not-for-profit, nonsectar-ian training organization, at www.iblp.org.

5. Bill Gothard, Institute in Basic Youth Conflicts, *Research in Principles of Life* (Oak Brook, IL: 1972).

6. See http://theheartofHolly.blogspot.com.

7. "Quick Facts," The American Society for Aesthetic Plastic Surgery, 2009. http://www.sur gery.org/sites/default/files/2009quickfacts.pdf.

Chapter 5: Searching for the Greater Good: The Stem Cell Debate

1. Charles Krauthammer, "Why Lines Must be Drawn," *TIME* magazine, August 23, 2004.

2. "Stem Cells to Cure Children of Chronic Liver Disease," *The Times of India,* March 21, 2010. http://timesofindia.indiatimes.com/home/science/Stem-cells-to-cure-children-of-chronic-liver-disease/articleshow/5708226.cms.

3. *Lives in the Balance: The Stem Cell Debate,* Joni and Friends TV episodes, DVDTV22.

4. Breakpoint with Charles Colson, "Human Life—It's What Matters Most," October 26, 2004.

5. "Cord Blood Stem Cells Reverse Girl's Cerebral Palsy," FOX News, July 28, 2008. http://www.FoxNews.com/story/0.2933.392061.00.html.

6. As a side note, there is an effort to legally lift the current restrictions, which forbid bring-ing a cloned embryo to nearly full term. That way, your cloned fetus would have com-pletely developed a liver, thereby serving as an exact match. Unfortunately for your clone, it would have to be aborted to harvest the organ tissues for your liver.

7. James P. Kelly, testimony before the Florida Senate Committee on Health Care, April 15, 2003.

Chapter 6: The Truth Behind the Pain of Abortion

1. Jeffrey Stinson, "Abortion Debate Gains Volume in Europe," *USA Today,* February 9, 2007. http://www.usatoday.com/news/world/2007-02-07-euroabortion_x.htm.

2. Michelle Malkin, "Planned Parenthood's Obscene Profits," MichelleMalkin.com, June 4, 2008. http://michellemalkin.com/2008/06/04/planned-parenthoods-obscene-profits/.

3. Resources available at www.saveone.org.

4. Subcommittee on Separation of Powers to Senate Judiciary Committee, S-158, 97th Congress, 1st Session, 1981.

5. *Doe v. Bolton,* 410 U.S. 179 (1973), Wikipedia.com. http://en.wikipedia.org/wiki/Doe_v._Bolton#Definition_of_health.

6. Ibid.

7. Joni and Friends, "Holding on to Hope," featuring David and Nancy Guthrie, DVDTV11. http://www.joniandfriends.tv.org

8. Ibid.

Chapter 7: A Calloused Conscience: Eugenics and Genocide

1. Courtney Taylor, "Parents of Down Syndrome Children Divorce Less: Study," *The Reporter,* Vanderbilt Medical Center's Weekly Newspaper, February 11, 2008. http://www.mc.vanderbilt.edu/reporter/index.html?ID=6087.

2. Susan W. Enouen, PE, "Down Syndrome and Abortion," *Physicians for Life,* 2010.

3. Ibid.

4. Alexander Graham Bell, "Memoir Upon the Formation of a Deaf Variety of the Human Race," 1883.

5. The history of eugenics in the United States is discussed at length in Mark Haller, *Eugenics: Hereditarian Attitudes in American Thought* (New Brunswick, NJ: Rutgers University Press, 1963), and Daniel Kevles, *In the Name of Eugenics: Genetics and the Uses of Human Heredity* (New York: Knopf, 1985), the latter being the standard survey work on the subject.

6. The connections between U.S. and Nazi eugenicists is discussed in Edwin Black, "Eugenics and the Nazis—the California Connection," *San Francisco Chronicle,* November 9, 2003, as well as Black's *War Against the Weak* (New York: Four Wars Eight Windows, 2003).

7. "Handicapped" brochure published by United States Holocaust Memorial Museum, Washington, DC, 2009.

8. Ohio Right to Life, 1982 press statement, Columbus, Ohio.

9. "Case Study: Female Infanticide," Gendercide Watch. http://gendercide.org/case_infanticide.html.

10. Wesley J. Smith, "Pushing Infanticide: From Holland to New Jersey," *The National Review,* March 22, 2005.

11. Dr. Peter H. Gott, "The Toll of Alzheimer's Disease," *Sunday News,* Lancaster, Pennsylvania, March 28, 2004.

12. Stephanie Hubach, "The Dignity of Every Human," *byFaith* Magazine, December 2006, no. 12, pp. 20-23.

13. Ibid., p. 4.

14. Dan Allender, *Leading with a Limp* (Colorado Springs, CO: WaterBrook Press, 2006), pp. 46,48.

15. Hugh Gregory Gallagher, *By Trust Betrayed: Patients, Physicians, and the License to Kill in the Third Reich,* rev. ed. (St. Petersburg, FL: Vandamere Press, 1995).

Chapter 8: From Obscurity to Celebrity by Way of Tragedy: End-of-Life Issues

1. "Man 'Trapped in Coma' for 23 Years Was Awake Whole Time," FOX News, November 23, 2009. http://www.foxnews.com/story/0,2933,576311,00.html.
2. Lawrence O. Gostin, JD, "Ethics, the Constitution and the Dying Process," *The Journal of the American Medical Association*, May 18, 2005, vol. 293, no. 19, p. 2403. http://jama.ama-assn.org/cgi/content/extract/293/19/2403.
3. Paul McHugh, "Annihilated Terri Schiavo," *Commentary*, June 2005, p. 29.
4. Ibid., p. 32.
5. James J. Walter, PhD, "Five Unacknowledged Shifts in the Catholic Tradition," Consortium of Jesuit Biotheics Programs' Symposium on Artificial Nutrition and Hydration. http://www.jesuitbioethics.net/files/JWalter_1208.pdf.
6. Henry Bavinck, *Reformed Dogmaticsy* (Grand Rapids, MI: Baker Academic, 2004), p. 115.
7. Other works used for this chapter include Gregory Pence's *Classic Cases in Medical Ethics* (Boston, MA: McGraw Hill, 2004) and *The Elements of Bioethics* (Boston, MA: McGraw Hill, 2007). I am also indebted to Dr. James Walter, Director of the Center of Bioethics at Loyola Marymount, for his incredible insight on artificial nutrition and hydration and quality-of-life judgments. Much of the materials in this chapter on these subjects were drawn from his lectures and notes.

Chapter 9: I've Got Questions About the American Dream

1. "Over Shopping and Over Spending Facts," The Shulman Center for Compulsive Theft and Spending. http://www.theshulmancenter.com/facts.htm#overshopping.
2. Juliet B. Schor, *Born to Buy: The Commercialized Child and the New Consumer Culture* (New York: Scribner, 2004).
3. Ibid.
4. Ibid.
5. Rachel Oliver, "All About Food Waste," CNN, January 22, 2008. http://edition.cnn.com/2007/WORLD/asiapcf/09/24/food.leftovers/index.html.
6. Paula Minahan, "Food Indulgence in America: How Attitudes Weigh Us Down," KABC-TV, Los Angeles, California, January 23, 2009. http://www.greenrightnow.com/kabc.
7. "Consumerism in America," University of Southern Maine. http://www.usm.maine.edu/~kuzma/security/projects/2002/alexander/consumerism.htm.
8. "Shopping Fever," EcoFuture.com. http://www.ecofuture.org/pk/pkar9506.html.
9. Ibid.
10. Ibid.
11. Anup Shah, "Consumption and Consumerism," Global Issues, September 3, 2008. http://www.globalissues.org/issue/235/consumption-and-consumerism.
12. Joni and Friends, "I've Got Questions," featuring Nick Vujicic, DVDTV08. http://www.joniandfriendstv.org.

Chapter 10: Now What?

1. Dan Allender, *Leading with a Limp* (Colorado Springs, CO: WaterBrook Press, 2006), p. 54.
2. From *Guerrillas of Grace*, copyright © 1984, 2005, Ted Loder, admin. Augsburg Fortress, p. 109. Reproduced by permission of Augsburg Fortress Publishers.

Appendix A: The Manhattan Declaration

1. Copyright © 2009 Manhattan Declaration. All rights reserved. Used with permission. http://www.ManhattanDeclaration.org.

Contributors

Steve Bundy is the Managing Director of the Christian Institute on Disability as well as International Outreach at Joni and Friends. This initiative paves the way for increased education, training and equipping of disability ministers while focusing on public policy issues that affect the disabled in our culture and world today. Steve frequently appears on *Joni and Friends* television episodes and has written articles or been interviewed for *Christianity Today, Charisma* magazine, Focus on the Family, and others.

Steve and his wife, Melissa, know firsthand the joys and challenges of parenting a child with special needs, as their own son, Caleb, was born with chromosome deletion, which resulted in global delay and a secondary diagnosis of autism. Steve holds a B.A. in Theology and Missions and an M.A. in Organizational Leadership. He is an ordained minister and has served as a youth pastor and missionary. Steve and Melissa have two sons and live in Simi Valley, California.

Sheila Harper is the Founder and President of SaveOne, an international outreach ministry for men and women suffering in silence after an abortion. After enduring seven years of anguish over choosing abortion, Sheila found forgiveness and restoration through Jesus Christ. She is the author of four books, including her personal story, *The Survivor*, and *SaveOne: A Guide to Emotional Healing After Abortion*, which has been translated into six languages. She speaks worldwide on the topic of abortion, while training recovery group facilitators.

SaveOne currently has 150 chapters in the U.S. and 20 international chapters in nine countries. She holds a B.A. in life-issues counseling and lives in Nashville, Tennessee, with her husband, Jack Harper, Pastor of CrossRoads Church in Antioch, Tennessee, and their two sons. You can order Sheila's books or find a SaveOne chapter near you at www.saveone.org.

Kathy McReynolds is the Director of Public Policy for the Joni and Friends Christian Institute on Disability. She develops position papers on bioethics that seek to benefit people with disabilities, as well as contributes to curriculum development for courses in disability studies.

Kathy holds a B.A. in Christian Education from Biola University, an M.A. in Systematic Theology from the Talbot School of Theology, and earned her Ph.D in Ethics at USC. She specializes in ethical issues in genetic enhancement research and has written five books. Since 2000, Kathy has taught in the Biblical Studies Department and the English and Apologetics Departments at Biola University. Kathy has served on several ethics committees for hospitals and universities, and has numerous prestigious awards, including the Leading Health Care Professional of the World by the International Biographical Center in 2009. Kathy resides in Oak Park, California, with her husband, Mike, and their three children.

Joni Eareckson Tada, the founder and Chief Executive Officer of Joni and Friends, is an international advocate for people with disabilities. A diving accident in 1967 left Joni, then 17, a quadriplegic in a wheelchair, unable to use her hands. Joni learned to paint with a brush between her teeth, and her art paintings and prints have become sought-after and collected.

Joni has served as an advisor on numerous committees, including the National Council on Disability and the Disability Advisory Committee to the U.S. State Department. Joni has received numerous awards, honors and honorary degrees. She's written 46 books and numerous magazine articles. Her best-selling autobiography, *Joni,* has been translated into many languages. She hosts *Joni and Friends,* a daily radio program, and the television version of *Joni and Friends* looks at people who inspire Joni by enduring the most difficult trials while continuing to trust in God. She has been featured in a variety of national publications, as well as television and radio programs. Joni and her husband, Ken Tada, have been married since 1982 and live in Calabasas, California.

Pat Verbal is the Manager of Curriculum Development at Joni and Friends Christian Institute on Disability. She is a featured speaker in churches, conferences and in the media, sharing from her 25 years of experience as a Christian education pastor, school administrator and consultant. Pat has written and/or co-authored 12 books and numerous articles on Christian education, including *Special Needs Special Ministry* and *Special Needs Smart Pages* by Joni and Friends.

In her work on the National Day of Prayer Task Force, Pat co-authored the best-selling *My Family's Prayer Calendar* with Shirley Dobson. She has been a guest on *Pastor to Pastor* from Focus on the Family, Trinity Broadcast Network, and a teacher for the Billy Graham School of Evangelism. She is a graduate of Azusa Pacific University and holds an M.A. in Pastoral Studies from the C. P. Haggard School of Theology, where she served on the Council of Church Leaders. Pat and her husband, Stan, have two grown sons and live in Dallas, Texas.

Scripture Index

Old Testament
Genesis 1:26-27; 97
Genesis 1:26-28; 165
Genesis 1:27; 141
Genesis 2:9; 104
Genesis 3; 172, 179
Genesis 3:22-24; 104
Genesis 4:6; 41
Genesis 5:1; 97
Genesis 5:1-3; 165
Genesis 9:6; 97, 165
Genesis 32:25-32; 142
Genesis 50:20; 143
Exodus 20:13; 15
Deuteronomy 10:18; 143
Deuteronomy 30:16-20; 204
Joshua 24:15; 64
Judges 17:6; 138
Judges 21:25; 206
1 Samuel 2:6; 121
1 Samuel 16:7; 82
Psalm 9:11-12; 143
Psalm 10:2; 143
Psalm 10:17; 143, 195
Psalm 10:17-18; 143
Psalm 22:24; 143
Psalm 27:1; 33
Psalm 37:4; 16
Psalm 82:3-4; 144, 193
Psalm 138:8; 84
Psalm 139:13; 97, 136, 143
Psalm 139:13-14; 115
Psalm 139:14; 129
Psalm 139:14-16; 86, 97, 164
Psalm 139:23-24; 181
Psalm 142:4; 64
Proverbs 2:1-5; 19
Proverbs 13:34; 193
Proverbs 14:12; 103
Proverbs 14:34; 193
Proverbs 15:13; 82, 86
Proverbs 16:9; 122
Proverbs 18:21; 76

Proverbs 22:6; 58
Proverbs 23:7; 72
Proverbs 24:3-4; 61
Proverbs 31:8-9; 145, 207
Proverbs 31:8; 25
Proverbs 31:9; 14
Ecclesiastes 8:11; 120
Isaiah 45:9; 86
Jeremiah 1:5; 164
Jeremiah 9:23-24; 186, 204
Jeremiah 18:6; 164
Jeremiah 29:11; 43, 121
Ezekiel 11:19-20; 205
Ezekiel 18:20; 120
Daniel 12:4; 104, 106
Micah 6:8; 193
Zechariah 2:8-9; 143

New Testament
Matthew 5:9; 50
Matthew 5:13; 50
Matthew 5:14; 50
Matthew 6:9-10; 194
Matthew 6:12; 49
Matthew 6:14-15; 41
Matthew 6:24; 179
Matthew 6:27; 83
Matthew 6:28; 83
Matthew 6:31-33; 184
Matthew 11:12; 194
Matthew 19:13-15; 55
Matthew 19:22; 179
Matthew 20:28; 142
Matthew 22:15-21; 185
Matthew 25:40; 141
Matthew 26:39; 122
Matthew 28:19-20; 67
Mark 10:46-52; 202
Mark 11:25; 41
Luke 12:11-12; 203
Luke 12:48; 185
Luke 14:12-14; 202
Luke 14:13-14; 187

Luke 23:34; 48
John 1:14; 166
John 8:44; 146
John 10:10; 129
John 13:35; 50
John 16:33; 38
Acts 10:38; 146
Acts 16:25-26; 125
Acts 26:18; 194
Romans 5:3; 38, 45
Romans 5:12; 172
Romans 8:15-17; 184
Romans 8:28; 143
Romans 8:29; 167
Romans 9:20; 86
Romans 9:21; 164
Romans 12:1-2; 190
Romans 12:2; 177
Romans 12:5; 62
Romans 12:19; 48
Romans 13:10; 167
Romans 14:17; 193
1 Corinthians 1:20,27; 203
1 Corinthians 1:26; 201
1 Corinthians 1:26-27; 59
1 Corinthians 1:27-29; 147
1 Corinthians 12:21; 144
1 Corinthians 12:22-24; 144
1 Corinthians 13:4-7; 187
1 Corinthians 13:12; 56
2 Corinthians 3:18; 167
2 Corinthians 4:4; 166
2 Corinthians 4:17; 45
2 Corinthians 5:20; 164
2 Corinthians 9:7; 187
2 Corinthians 12:9; 86
2 Corinthians 12:11; 144
Galatians 5:14; 167
Galatians 6:10; 196
Ephesians 1:1-14; 181
Ephesians 1:4-5; 183
Ephesians 1:11; 143
Ephesians 2:10; 80, 84, 86
Ephesians 4:15; 19
Ephesians 4:22-24; 167
Ephesians 4:26; 41
Ephesians 4:32; 61

Ephesians 5:1; 165
Ephesians 5:1-2; 167
Ephesians 5:11-13; 19
Ephesians 6:12; 146
Philippians 2:6-7; 188
Philippians 2:13; 44, 127
Philippians 3:1-11; 181
Colossians 1:15; 166
Colossians 1:21; 165
Colossians 2:9-10; 180
Colossians 3:3; 190
Colossians 3:3-4; 89
Colossians 3:9-10; 167
Colossians 3:14; 167
Colossians 4:5-6; 199
1 Timothy 4:12; 199
1 Timothy 6:6; 176
1 Timothy 6:9-10; 176
1 Timothy 6:10; 178
Hebrews 1:3; 140
Hebrews 12:2; 83, 90
Hebrews 12:14; 193, 194
Hebrews 12:15; 44
Hebrews 13:21; 31
James 1:2; 37
James 1:2-3; 56
James 1:5-6; 18
James 1:9; 145
James 1:14-15; 173
James 1:19-20; 41
James 1:22; 195
James 2:14-17; 189
James 3:5-12; 76
James 3:9; 97, 166
James 4:11; 61
1 Peter 1:6; 46
1 Peter 2:21; 16
1 Peter 3:3-4; 86
1 Peter 3:15; 14
1 John 2:16; 87, 179
1 John 2:16-17; 87, 88
1 John 4:19; 186
1 John 5:19; 194
Revelation 1:18; 194
Revelation 11:15; 195
Revelation 12:10; 146
Revelation 13:6; 146

Great Resources from

www.joniandfriends.org

PO Box 3333 • Agoura Hills, CA 91376
(818) 707-5664 • Fax: (818) 707-2391 • TTY: (818) 707-9707

Making Sense of Autism: Part 1 & Part 2
By Joni and Friends

Autism is on the rise in America. But its causes remain unknown, and a cure is yet to be found. Common misunderstandings include the notions that children with autism are not able to learn or that their behavior is simply the result of poor discipline. In Part One, we will dispel these myths, as we look into the lives of families that live with autism. Part Two addresses the role of the church in the lives of these families. We'll find out what they need most from the church as well as the blessings that come from including everyone in the Body of Christ. Study guides are also included.

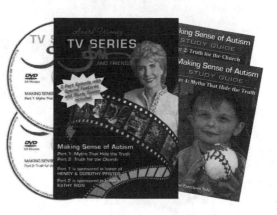

2 DVDs – 28 Minutes Each
Code: DVDTV30 $15.95

How to Be a Christian in a Brave New World
By Joni Eareckson Tada and Nigel M. de S. Cameron

Stem-cell research. Cloning. Genetic engineering. Discoveries in biotechnology occur so rapidly that we can barely begin to address one ethical debate before another looms overhead. This brave new world that we've entered is a daunting one with disturbing implications for the sanctity of life. How should we respond as Christians? Here is passionate, gripping reading about the world that is already here, and how to live out your faith with conviction in its midst.

Softcover – 208 Pages
Code: BK057 $17.00

Certification Course: *Beyond Suffering: Christian Views on Disability Ministry*

This 32-hour certification program is designed to give participants an introductory understanding of the aspects of disability ministry. The program presents four thought-provoking models:

• *Overview of Disability Ministry* • *Theology of Disability* • *Church and Disability* • *Introduction to Bioethics*

Participants learn through lectures, group discussions, video, and hands-on experiences to welcome, evangelize, and empower people affected by disability into the church. This program is designed for ministers, professionals, teachers, and volunteers. For more information call 818-707-5664 or visit us online at: www.joniandfriends.org/CID.